Revolution in Iran: A Reappraisal

Edited by
Enver M. Koury
and
Charles G. MacDonald

The directors of the Institute of Middle Eastern
and African Affairs
Welcome the submission of manuscripts
relevant to the Middle East and Africa.
Manuscripts submitted for publication
must be prepared in double-spaced typescript.
Footnotes should be placed at the end of the text.
It is essential that three copies of the manuscript be submitted.

For information, write Institute of Middle Eastern and
North African Affairs, Inc.,
P.O. Box 1674
Hyattsville, Maryland, 20788

The views expressed in the institute's publications are those of the authors
and do not necessarily reflect the views of the staff or advisory board
of the Institute of Middle Eastern and North African Affairs.

Copyright © 1982 by the Institute of Middle Eastern
and North African Affairs (Inc.)

All right reserved. No part of this book may be reproduced in any form
or by any electronic or mechanical means including information storage
and retrieval systems without permission in writing from the author or
the Institute except by a reviewer who may quote brief passages in a
review.

Library of Congress Catalog Card Number 81-85470
ISBN 0-934484-16-3

DS
316.8
R 48
1982

CONTRIBUTORS

ROBERT G. DARIUS is a faculty member at the Strategic Studies Institute, U.S. Army War College, Carlisle Barracks, Pennsylvania. He earned an A.B. from Glenville State College, an M.A. from American University, and a Ph.D. in Political Science from the University of Maryland. He has taught in the Interdisciplinary Social Sciences Program at the University of Maryland and has served as a Research-Associate at the Institute for International Political and Economic Studies, Tehran, Iran. His published works include *American Diplomacy: An Option Analysis of the Azerbaijan Crisis, 1946-46* [1978]; *Iran's Foreign Policy, 1941-1974: A Selective Bibliography*, compiled with Fereshteh Ashraf [1976]; and several articles in English and Farsi for professional journals.

LISA M. deFILIPPIS is a graduate student in the Woodrow Wilson Department of Government and Foreign Affairs, University of Virginia. Her thesis topic is "U.S. Policy in the Persian Gulf." She received a B.A. with Distinction from the University of Virginia in 1977. In the summers of 1976 and 1977 she served as an administrative assistant in the Department of State, Bureau of Near East and South Asia, Public Affairs Office, and worked on the Bureau Task Force during the Lebanese crisis in 1976. She wrote *An Annotated Guide to the Middle East Materials in Alderman Library* (University of Virginia) and a subsequent *Supplement*.

ENVER M. KOURY is Associate Professor of Government and Politics at the University of Maryland and General Director of the Institute of Middle Eastern and North African Affairs. He was born in the United States but was reared in Lebanon. He has lived in various parts of the Middle East and North Africa and has travelled extensively throughout the area. He is the author of *The Patterns of Mass Movements in Arab Revolutionary-Progressive States; The Superpowers and the Balance of Powers in the Arab World; The Operational Capability of the Lebanese Political System; Oil and Geopolitics in the Persian Gulf Area: A Center of Power; The Middle East and North Africa: Definition and Analysis of Regional Balances of Power; The Balance of Economic Power: North-South Confrontation on Raw Materials; The Crisis in the Lebanese System: Confessionalism and Chaos; The Balance of Military Power: The Arab-Israeli Conflict; The Saudi Decision-Making Body: The House of Al-Saud; The Arabian Peninsula, Red Sea, and Gulf: Strategic Considerations;* and *The United Arab Emirates: Its Political System and Politics.*

CHARLES G. MACDONALD is Assistant Professor of International Relations at Florida International University in North Miami, Florida. During the 1979-80 academic year he held a visiting appointment in the Woodrow Wilson Department of Government and Foreign Affairs at the University of Virginia. He earned his B.A. at Florida State University and his M.A. and Ph.D. in Foreign Affairs at the University of Virginia. He is author of *Iran, Saudi Arabia, and the Law of the Sea* (1980). He is currently writing *Frantz Fanon and the Iranian Revolution: The Search for Self-Esteem in the Third World*. His articles have appeared in *Middle East Journal, Naval War College Review, Journal of South Asian and Middle Eastern Studies,* and *Levant* (Pakistan).

ROUHOLLAH K. RAMAZANI is Chairman and Edward R. Stettinius Professor, Woodrow Wilson Department of Government and Foreign Affairs, University of Virginia. Formerly the Vice-President of the American Institute of Iranian Studies, he has been the Aga Khan Professor of Islamic Studies at the American University of Beirut; Visiting Professor of Middle Eastern Studies at the School of Advanced International Studies of The Johns Hopkins University; and Visiting Member of the High Table at King's College, Cambridge University, England. His most recent books include: *The Persian Gulf: Iran's Role [1972]; Iran's Foreign Policy 1941-1973: A Study of Foreign Policy in Modernizing Nations [1975]; Beyond the Arab-Israeli Settlement: New Directions for U.S. Policy in the Middle East [1977]; and The Persian Gulf and the Strait of Hormuz [1979].* He is currently writing *U.S.-Iran Influence Relationship* and is also working on "The Socio-Political Dimensions of Access to Persian Gulf Oil."

TABLE OF CONTENTS

		Page
	CONTRIBUTORS	III
	PREFACE	VII
I.	**IRAN'S FOREIGN POLICY: PERSPECTIVES AND PROJECTIONS** *Rouhollah K. Ramazani*	9
II.	**THE IRANIAN REVOLUTION OF 1978-79: POTENTIAL IMPLICATIONS FOR MAJOR COUNTRIES IN THE AREA** *Robert Ghobad Darius*	30
III.	**IRAN AS A POLITICAL VARIABLE: PATTERNS AND PROSPECTS** *Charles G. MacDonald*	49
IV.	**THE AYATOLLAH REVOLUTION: LACK OF CONSENSUS ON FUNDAMENTALS** *Enver M. Koury*	61
V.	**U.S. SECURITY IN THE PERSIAN GULF: AN ASSESSMENT** *Lisa deFilippis*	88
VI.	**REACTIONS TO IRAN'S REVOLUTION: THE SEARCH FOR SECURITY** *Charles G. MacDonald*	98

PREFACE

The aim of this work is to examine the Iranian Revolution in a dispassionate manner, with a view to understanding better the nature of the revolution and its implications. The articles were selected to offer a variety of perspectives on the revolution and on reactions to it; to provide insights into the dynamics of Iran's internal power struggle; and to project Iran's foreign policy options as determined by the complex political conflicts found in the Gulf.

In the first chapter Rouhollah K. Ramazani masterfully places the Iranian Revolution into historical perspective by focusing on alternative periods of crisis and tranquility in the twentieth century. He identifies the revolution as the sixth Iranian crisis of the century. Next, Robert G. Darius provides an analysis of the revolution and its implications as were evident in mid 1979. His study draws from observations of other Iranian specialists and from insights based upon his own Iranian experiences. In chapter three Charles G. MacDonald examines the political dynamics of the Gulf that establish parameters for projecting the foreign policy of revolutionary Iran. He also focuses upon certain internal political developments that shed light upon Iranian efforts to export revolution.

In the fourth chapter Enver M. Koury's study of the internal workings of Iran's pluralistic political system provides keen insights into Iran's ongoing power struggle and a genuine appreciation of Iran's political mosaic. He explores the internal political dynamics of Iran that are also characteristic of other fragmented Middle Eastern societies, such as Lebanon.

In the fifth chapter Lisa M. deFilippis critically analyzes American policy toward the Gulf, the problems it has encountered, and its reevaluation following the fall of the Shah. She views U.S. Gulf policy as reflecting two basic strategies—containment and regional partnership—and emphasizes the need for a "balanced" policy that encourages security cooperation among the Gulf States.

In the final chapter Charles G. MacDonald examines the search for security by key Middle Eastern states in the aftermath of the Iranian Revolution. He observes that the policies adopted seek to strengthen defenses and to foster the legitimacy of the respective governments in response to the new revolutionary pressures.

It is hoped that this work will be beneficial, not only to Middle East specialists, but also to government officials and students, by providing a better understanding of both the Iranian Revolution and its significance in the Gulf and beyond.

I. IRAN'S FOREIGN POLICY: PERSPECTIVES AND PROJECTIONS *

Rouhollah K. Ramazani

On the eve of the New Year 1978 President Carter told the Shah in Teheran that Iran was an "island of stability." The President might also have added that Iran was perceived to be the most powerful state in the Persian Gulf; a leading regional power in the adjacent areas of the Middle East, South Asia and the Horn of Africa; and a potential middle power in world politics. By the end of that same year, however, Iran was teetering on the verge of economic collapse, threatened by political chaos, and rapidly losing its capacity in world politics. In January the Shah left Iran, never to return.

The Shah's foreign policy was in shambles even before he left Iran. Before taking office, his last Prime Minister, Dr. Shapur Bakhtiar, told American officials that Iran should no longer play the "policeman" role in the Persian Gulf. Few observers believed that the massive purchase orders of arms from the United States would be carried out; that plans for the construction by 1994 of some twenty nuclear power stations with French, German, and American assistance would be implemented; or that numerous civilian projects, involving billions of dollars' transactions with foreign firms, would survive the crisis.

Within months after the revolutionary seizure of power, United States interests in Iran, nurtured over the nearly four decades of the Shah's regime, seemed in jeopardy. Some $6 billion of American exports to Iran in the year preceding the revolution was lost. The number of American citizens in iran was reduced from around 45,000 to about 3,000.

To assess the impact of the revolution on the course of Iran's foreign policy requires deep understanding of its past foreign policy experience under both stable and unstable conditions. That experience goes far back in centuries, but only its manifestations in the twentieth century should concern us here. The current revolutionary crisis is actually the

---

*Adapted from "Iran's Foreign Policy: Perspectives and Projections," in *Economic Consequences of the Revolution in Iran: A Compendium of Papers*, submitted to the U.S. Congress Joint Economic Committee, 96th Congress, 1st Session, November 19, 1979 (Washington, D.C.: U.S. Government Printing Office, 1980), pp. 65-97.

sixth one of its kind and this century, and it has much in common with the five that preceded it. An examination of the other five religio-nationalist crises should, therefore, provide perspective on Iran's future foreign policy—assuming that the present unstable conditions persist. In the event stability is achieved, Iran's foreign policy experience in tranquil conditions during three stable periods of this century also will be examined.

For purposes of this study political periods in Iranian history from 1905 to the 1978 revolution can be divided as follows:

Crisis	Tranquility	Summary of events
1905 to 1914		The constitutional revolution.
1914 to 1921		Foreign military intervention.
	1921 to 1941	The rule of Reza Khan.
1941 to 1951		World War II and its aftermath.
1951 to 1953		Nationalism and internal political strife.
	1954 to 1961	An enforced tranquility: increased ties with the United States.
1961 to 1964		Foreign pressures and political reform.
	1964 to 1978	An artificial calm before the revolution

The Evolution of Iranian Foreign Policy During Alternative Periods of Crisis and Tranquility

I. (1905-1914) *The First Crisis: The Constitutional Revolution*

Iran's capacity for effective action in international affairs was reduced to a minimum during the first crisis of the century (1905-1914). The constitutional revolution that marked the beginning of the crisis period theoretically ended with the forced adjournment of the Second Majlis (second parliamentary session) in 1911, but internal and external forces of instability prevailed until the outbreak of World War I and the beginning of a new crisis.

The revolution was rooted in widespread religious and lay dissatisfaction with the consequences of domestic and foreign policies of the Qajar dynasty, particularly during the fiteen years preceding the outbreak of the crisis. Oppsition to the Qajar monarch at the time was supported by some of the religious leaders (the ulama), elements of the modern-educated groups, and sections of the Bazaar merchants. The reasons and rationales for the opposition were mixed and found expression in the cry of Islam, liberty, and independence. For the ulama royal attempts at secularization and perceived domination by the secular element posed a threat to Islam and, of course, to their clerical power and interests. For the educated intellectuals the overriding perceived threat lay in foreign control and internal tyranny, both regarded as detrimental to their ideals and their share of political power. Bazaar merchants feared increasing encroachment on their economic interest and on their attachment to Islam by the government and the newly emerging entrepreneurial class.

Throughout the crisis period no single group or individual controlled the government, and the government was incapable of maintaining central power over the provinces. The first two sessions of the Majlis were destroyed in the struggle between constitutionalists and royalists, each side supported by different armed groups, such as the Mujahedin (Muslim fighters) and the Bakhtiari tribesmen who helped the nationalists and the Russian-commanded Cossack Division that stayed with the Shah.

During the period external, no less than internal, conditions sapped Iran's capacity for action in foreign affairs. The Russians helped to close the Majlis by naked military intervention. No cabinet was formed or dispersed without Anglo-Russian interference. In Iran the Russians and the British set aside their traditional rivalry in their common efforts against the extension of German power in the Middle East; they divided Iran into spheres of influence by a convention signed in 1907.

The government's capacity in foreign affairs was reduced to rhetorical opposition to the great powers. The Majlis did hire an American financial adviser, Morgan Shuster, but even this, the single major foreign policy decision of the constitutional regime, was foiled by Russian intervention with British acquiescence.

II. (1914-1912) *World War I and Foreign Military Intervention*

Iran's capacity for action in international affairs was as limited during the second crisis period as it was in the first. Unlike the first, the second was the product of foreign military intervention. It was triggered by World War I.

The same internal factors that had characterized the first crisis prevailed after 1914, but they were aggravated during the second crisis. There was no unified power center in government. Seventeen-year-old Ahmad Shah spent his time abroad, as had the Regent before him, thus removing a possible element of stability. The deputies of the Third Majlis were dispersed between Teheran and Qom and divided between the "Moderates" and the "Democrats." Cabinets rose and fell with sensational speed in conjunction with the factional and personal struggles for power and the vicissitudes of the war.

Iran's territorial integrity was in jeopardy, not only because of battling foreign troops on its soil, but also because of various tribal, provincial and ethnic uprisings.

The government (or rather governments) was virtually unable to maintain the polity of neutrality that had been proclaimed by Prime Minister Mostowfi al-Mamalik at the outset of the war. The dispersed deputies of the Majlis, most of the Democrats and some of the Moderates, openly sided with the Central Powers, and their armed supporters fought internal battles, with German and Turkish aid, against Russian forces on Iran's territory. The major tribes (Bakhtiaris, Qashqa'is, Baluchis, Hazaras and the Khamsah) all took up arms in favor of one or another foreign power. The Azerbaijani Mujahedin sided with the Turks, and the followers of the Bolshevik-supported Jangali movement fought against the British forces.

III. (1921-1941) *A Period of Tranquility Under Reza Khan*

The first period of tranquility stretched from Reza Khan's military coup in 1921 until his abdication in 1941. Iran's increasing capacity for effective action in foreign affairs resulted from a combination of imposed tranquility and favorable external environment.

Domestic tranquility was achieved step by step through the imposition of authoritarian control over the government and the entire political system. First, Reza Khan managed to control, unify and strengthen the motley armed forces inherited from the past. The only force then in existence was the Cossack Division which, as Army Chief, he commanded after the coup. He outmaneuvered two Prime Ministers, Sayyed Zia and Ahmad Qavam, in order to control the Ministery of War and to bring the Gendarmerie and the police under its jurisdiction. Second, he established central government over rebellious provinces, mainly by the force of arms. In Azerbaijan, for example, he crushed the local Gendarmerie forces led by Lahuti Khan and the Kurds led by Simko. He also destroyed the Bolshevik-supported Republic of Gilan led by Mirza Kuchek Khan. Third, he appeased and then controlled the religious leaders by a complete *volte-face* in the city of Qom where his idea of establishing a "Republic" as in Turkey was opposed. Finally, he cajoled and outmaneuvered his political opponents, such as the clerical deputy Muddares and the nationalist Mussaddiq, in the Fourth Majlis. He also overcame the power of such veteran statesmen as Qavam, Mostowfi and Mushir ed-Dowleh in the Cabinet, Eventually he was installed as the Shah and founder of the Pahlevi dynasty by the Fifth Majlis.

Iran's capacity for effective action in foreign affairs under the Shah was as much the result of favorable external circumstances as it was of his ability to impose his will on the country. To date, the nationalists believe that the British government orchestrated the coup that swept him into power. Although this is not supported by historical evidence, there is no doubt that the British provided encouragement. Besides the generally benevolent attitude of the British, at least at the beginning, his regime was not opposed by the government of Russia. Soviet Russia, as well as Britain, favored a strong central government in Teheran. The Soviets were preoccupied with the problem of power consolidation, and the British, having failed to impose a protectorate on Iran before the coup, turned their attention to the post-war problems of the British empire.

Iran's increased capability in foreign affairs was attested by the Shah's ability to win an unprecedented degree of independence from Britain and the Soviet Union. The capitulations system was abolished; British control over southwestern Iran through the Arab leader Sheikh Khaza'l was largely eliminated; Russian colonization of northern Iran was ended; and relations with Turkey, Iraq, and Afghanistan were improved. The main failure of the Shah's British policy was that, although he canceled the British oil concession in 1932, he signed a new one for an even longer duration a year later. The main failure of his Russian policy was his inability to induce the Soviets to cancel their right of unilateral military intervention in Iran under the 1921 treaty.

In his quest to maintain his regime and simultaneously to resist British and Soviet pressures, the Shah relied upon Germany, both as a means of modernization and as a counterweight to the other two great powers. Neither the stability of his regime nor the capacity of Iran in world affairs could be maintained indefinitely by such means. His dictatorial control over the Majlis, the press, the political groupings, the trade unions and the educational system, for example, alienated the growing middle class and the politically awakened elements regardless of ideology. His forced secularization, ranging from the abolition of the veil to hasty and superficial adoption of numerous modern legal codes from the West, lacked sufficient concern for indigenous values, life-styles and traditions and alienated many different groups. His coercive sedentarization of tribal groups and the imposition of the Persian language on the Azeris, the Arabs, the Kurds, and other minorities as the universal medium of communication and learning further fueled the quest for autonomy rather than fostering national integration. His deep-seated sense of mistrust of the British, and more so the Russians, made his foreign policy vulnerable, because by the end of his rule he relied too heavily on Germany. The excessive German presence there was used as an excuse by the Allies for their invasion of Iran and hastened the downfall of the regime. Another period of increased international power, based largely on imposed domestic tranquility and fortuitous external circumstances, collapsed overnight.

IV. (1941-1951) *The Third Crisis: World War II and Its Aftermath*

The third crisis, like the second one, was sparked by foreign military intervention in Iran and lasted from 1941 to 1951. Quite apart from the Allied powers' need of Iran as a route for supplying arms to the Soviet Union in the prosecution of war against Germany, Reza Shah's own foreign policy contributed to the Allied invasion of Iran. The Shah underestimated the heightened Allied need for Iran's cooperation once Germany invaded the Soviet Union. The Shah's miscalculation was largely the result of his authoritarian rule and his dominant foreign policy-making role. Despite the Allied invasion and occupation of Iran, the Iranian capacity for formulating and implementing foreign policy decisions was not wholly destroyed, but it was considerably limited.

Twenty-two-year-old Mohammad Reza Shah assumed the throne in the wake of his father's abdication in 1941. He was aided by numerous experienced Prime Ministers, especially by Ahmad Qavam and for a very short period by General Razm-Ara. As a military man, he was trained far better than Ahmad Shah during World War I. He showed consistent determination to deepen and broaden American interests in Iran both as a means of strengthening his rule through military and economic modernization and as a device to resist British and Soviet pressure.

The abdication of Reza Shah resulted in a burst of relatively uncontrolled political activities. The liberal nationalist elements wishfully characterized the early post-Reza years as "the era of revived constitutionalism." After the release of political prisoners from the old Shah's prisons and the return of exiles, the nationalists competed with the communists and the Muslim fundamentalists for power. The Iran Party became the core of what later developed into the National Front, led by Dr. Mohammad Musaddiq. The Muslim fundamentalists gathered partly around the personality of Sayyed Abolghasem Kashani, a religious leader in exile, who returned to Iran. The communists assembled the well-organized Tudeh Party. While factionalism, cliquism, personalism as well as nationalism, Islam and communism permeated political activities, the net effect of these forces on the Majlis was for the most part positive. The Majlis emerged as an actor of some substance despite the surrounding chaos.

Another positive element on the scene was the increasing strength of the armed forces. The military had been dispersed, paralyzed and demoralized as a result of its humiliating defeat in attempting to resist the combined British and Russian forces that invaded Iran. Yet, the Shah's modernization efforts, aided by the United States, made it possible for the military to recover its strength rather rapidly. Its performance under the Shah's direct supervision against rebel forces in Azerbaijan and Kurdistan further added to its image. It must be stated, however, that the collapse of the rebel regimes was mainly the result of Ahmad Qavam's successful diplomacy with active British and particularly American support. Nevertheless, as a result of the weakness of the central government as well as the conditions of war and occupation, Iran's territorial integrity was threatened by provincial and tribal demands for autonomy. The Qashqa'is, the Kurds and the Azeris, especially the latter two, created difficult problems for maintaining domestic political stability and external security.

Although Iran's capacity for action in international politics was severely limited by internal divisions and external interference, a combination of skillful diplomacy and external support enabled the Iranian government to surmount the grave difficulties posed by the Soviet Union. In resisting Soviet pressures for oil concessions, the Shah and his Prime Minister were supported externally by the United States and internally by the right-wing nationalist leader, Sayyed Zia, and the veteran Iranian nationalist leader, Dr. Musaddiq. The pro-Soviet Tudeh party on the other hand vehemently opposed the government's oil policies in 1944 and again in 1947; in both instances the Soviets failed. The government's capacity for action was revealed in its successful efforts to pressure the Soviet Union to withdraw the Red Army troops from Iran and its support from the communist puppet regimes in Azerbaijan and Kurdistan. In this instance too, the internal and external forces combined in favor of the otherwise weak government of Iran. The Tudeh Party once again opposed the government's policies toward the Soviet Union, but the nationalist elements, Britain, and the United States supported it. These were classic examples of how an internally weakened government could nevertheless undertake foreign policy initiatives successfully as long as domestic and external support sustained its actions.

V. (1951-1953)) *The Fourth Crisis: Nationalization and Internal Political Strife*

While a combination of sufficient domestic and external support enabled Iran's weak government to act effectively during the third crisis, combined domestic and external opposition to the government's foreign policy led to its failure in the fourth crisis (1951-1953). Diverse political forces coalesced for a brief time under the leadership of Dr. Musaddiq, the leader of the National Front. These forces pushed laws through the Majlis for the nationalization of the Anglo-Iranian Oil Company (AIOC) against the resistance of the company, the British government, and the

Iranian government under the Shah and Prime Minister Razm-Ara. A handful of National Front deputies of the Majlis, who enjoyed widespread social support, defeated the government-supported supplementary oil agreement in the Sixteenth Majlis. Its Oil Commission, under the chairmanship of Dr. Musaddiq, initiated the adoption of the oil nationalization laws. Just before the enactment of the single-article principle of nationalization, Khalil Tahmasebi, a member of the militant Muslim Fedayeen, assassinated Prime Minister Razm-Ara. The Shah reluctantly appointed Dr. Mussaddiq as Prime Minister. The implementation of these nationalization laws was the most important foreign policy issue of his regime, since it involved the AIOC, the British government acting on behalf of the AIOC, and the United States initially serving as an "impartial" mediator between Iran, the AIOC, and the British. In the process, however, Dr. Musaddiq lost the capacity to implement his polities; mounting domestic and external opposition destroyed his regime in 1953.

Dr. Musaddiq's internal loss of support included all the major groups that had initially supported his crusade against the AIOC. The communist Tudeh Party supported him until he accepted President Truman's offer of Mr. Averell Harriman's mediation. The National Front itself split as some of Dr. Musaddiq's close associates became increasingly disenchanted with his solo performance and unproductive diplomatic battles with the AIOC and Britain. He also lost the support of a large segment of the religious elements as a result of differences with his former staunch supporter, Ayatollah Kashani. The Prime Minister's largest domestic problem, however, was the Shah. His efforts to weaken the Shah's powers in the name of the Constitution, particularly his abortive attempts to weaken the Shah's hold on the military through budgetary manipulation and finally through civilian control, sharpened the contest for power and led to the downfall of his regime.

Externally, Dr. Musaddiq's government lost the capacity to implement his nationalization policy because of the rise of foreign opposition that paralleled the erosion of his domestic support. There is no doubt that at the beginning of the crisis the United States viewed Dr. Mussadiq's government differently from the British. The Democratic Administration in the United States, especially Dean Acheson, the Secretary of State, counseled British as well as Iranian moderation in attempts to settle the prolonged dispute. The United States continued its technical assistance and military advisory programs in Iran and offered it mediation and good offices. The long-standing British call for the overthrow of the Musaddiq government eventually began to find a more sympathetic ear in Washington. This resulted from Dr. Musaddiq's inability to compromise with the British; the deteriorating economic conditions of Iran; the rise of the Tudeh power; the American Cold War fear of the possibility of a "communist coup" in Iran; and particularly the coming into power of the Conservatives in Britain and the Republicans in Washington. The CIA assisted the Shah and his supporters in overthrowing the Musaddiq government and returning the Shah to the country.

VI. (1953-1961) *An Enforced Tranquility: Increased Ties with the United States*

Iran's capacity in foreign affairs increased substantially between 1953 and 1961 as a result of imposed internal cooperation and favorable external support.

Mohammad Reza Shah, as his father, relied on a combination of naked force and military modernization to strengthen his regime after 1953. The Tudeh Party was suppressed by the arrest of some ninety-one communist dissidents in 1953, the destruction of the Tudeh network in the Army in 1954, the execution of Krusrow Ruzbeh (the so-called Lenin of Iran) in 1957 and similar acts. The National Frontists fared no better. Hussian Fatemi, Musaddiq's Foreign Minister, was executed. Activities of the National Resistance Movement were smashed. Mass arbitrary detention and imprisonment of nationalist elements followed. The death sentence of Mussaddiq was reduced to confinement. After 1957 the Shah's main instrument of repression and torture was the State Security and Intelligence Organization (SAVAK). It was established with the aid of the CIA and cooperated with Mossad, the Israeli intelligence service.

Iran's capacity for foreign policy action increased also because of external support of the regime by the United States in particular. As early as 1942 the Shah had begun to cultivate American friendship both as a means of strengthening his regime through military modernization and as a counterweight to the Soviet Union, the Shah's *bete noir*. American oil companies acquired a share in Iranian production for the first time in 1954 (40 percent); the United States was accorded an unprecedented opportunity for private investment and commerce in Iran under a treaty in 1957. American firms constituted about one-third of all foreign firms in Iran and accounted for more than a third of all the foreign capital invested outside oil before the Shah's fall in 1979.

Bolstered by an alliance with the United States, the Shah's regime demonstrated an increased capacity to deal with Soviet pressures and enticements. It responded favorably to Soviet overtures of "peaceful coexistence" by attempting to settle long-standing financial, boundary and commercial problems, and at the same time resisted Soviet pressures created by propaganda directed against Iran's alliance with the West and its favorable oil relations with multinational corporations under the international consortium agreement. The Shah's regional policies reflected both his alliance with the United States and his defiance of the Soviet Union. He tried to counter the power of the Nasser regime by cultivating friendship with the more conservative regimes in the Middle East. He also favored discreet relations with Israel, largely as a pro-Western and anti-Soviet power in the area.

VII. (1961-1964) *Foreign Pressures and Political Reform*

The Shah's domestic and foreign policies seemed in brief trouble in 1961 when the last crisis of the twentieth century before the current revolution broke out. It lasted until 1964 when the Ayatollah Rouhollah Khomeini was exiled. At first glance, the crisis seems a contradiction because it apparently resulted from the Shah's liberalizing of domestic politics. In fact, the Shah's attempt at so-called political liberalization was primarily in response to external pressures. Prospects of the Democrats' presidential success in the United States had worried the Shah. Once on office, President Kennedy categorically opposed further military aid to the Shah's regime and insisted on social and economic change. The Shah's choice of the reputedly pro-American reformist Dr. Ali Amini as Prime Minister was in deference to Washington, as was the Shah's short-lived tolerance of the National Front. The pressure from Moscow was far more severe. Soviet leader, Nikita Khrushchev, verbally attacked the Shah twice, blaming him for the breakdown of negotiations for a long-term nonaggression treaty between Teheran and Moscow that had started in 1958. He especially resented the Shah's conclusion in 1959 of a bilateral defense agreement with Washington in the wake of that breakdown in negotiations.

Token political liberalization emboldened the opposition and led to widespread teachers' strikes without impressing Washington or easing pressures for political permissiveness intended to help the Communists in Iran. There had to be a way of preventing a dangerous coalition of external and internal forces against the regime. The Shah's answer to the problem was a program of social and economic, rather than political, reforms and a new look into foreign affairs. At the time, and for a number of years afterwards, until the outbreak of the current revolution, both attempts seemed to pay off handsomely.

The Shah decided in September 1962 to pledge the Soviet Union that Iran would allow now foreign missile bases on its territory. The gesture was taken by both countries as a watershed of a new era in their relations. As a matter of fact, it caused an immediate change of Soviet attitude toward the Shah's regime. The Soviet propaganda machine immediately ceased its attacks on the regime; opponents of the Shah were decried as "reactionaries"; Iranian attempts at land reform, called a device to "strengthen the rotten monarchical regime" a few months earlier, were now characterized as "pioneering."

The Shah's decision to launch his land reform in January 1963 brought not only Soviet praise, but also that of President Kennedy. Domestically, however, it aroused the wrath of some of the religious leaders, especially the Ayatollah Khomeini. Once again nationalist and religious forces in alliance opposed the Shah's regime in a minor uprising in June 1963. They were crushed brutally by the royal government. When Khomeini spoke against the regime in 1964, his words were directed at the United States as well. Under the prodding of the U.S. Defense Department, the Majlis passed the Shah's bill to grant diplomatic immunity to American military personnel. The bill was seen by the Shah's opponents as an attempt to reestablish foreign capitulations that had existed for a century and had been abolished in 1928. Khomeini characterized the bill as a document that placed Iran under "American bondage." The Ayatollah's adamant refusal to be threatened or to moderate his opposition to the Shah's domestic or foreign policies led to his exile in 1964 from which he was not to return until after the Shah's exile in early 1979.

VIII. (1964-1978) An Artificial Era of Tranquility Brought About by Huge Oil Revenues: The Shah Fails to Take Advantage of his Opportunities.

Following these divisive events, Iran's international power potential and activity increased to an unprecedented degree between 1964 and the revolutionary crisis that began in 1978. It might appear paradoxical that the revolution should have followed such a period of domestic tranquility and international capability. However, it is necessary to understand the fragility of the Shah's regime on the one hand and its capability for effective international action on the other. Furthermore, a distinction must be made between the nature of the regime's strong international activity during 1964-67 and the turnabout during 1968-1978.

Domestically, the Shah's supression of the June 1963 uprising and the exile of Khomeini a year later marked the beginning of his efforts to consolidate power. The main tactics of political consolidation were the same as those of the 1950s—suppression of political opposition; control of party politics through the facade of a two-party system, previously through the Mardum and Mellyum Party and then through the Iran Novin and Mardum; control of the Majlis and the press; and the instrumentality of security forces, most particularly the SAVAK. The Shah's so-called "White Revolution," which began in response to foreign and domestic pressures, did for a short while contribute to an unprecedented rate of economic growth and such useful programs as the Literary Corps. There were, however, many shortcomings, most particularly a shortage of skilled manpower and a maldistribution of wealth. By 1967 some observers believed that Iran was reaching the economic "take-off" point. The United States, buoyed by the visible upturn in the Iranian economy, terminated its longstanding economic assistance program. Even a leftist critic of the Shah's regime observed subsequently that "whatever qualifications are made, there can be no doubt that Iran's record is both a substantial one and, in any comparative sense, exceptional. Iran, now one of the most developed such states (capitalist states), has had one of the highest sustained growth rates of any third-world country, capitalist or communist." [1]

Externally, the less polarized international environment in general and the superpowers' attitudes toward the Shah's regime aided its capability for a more active role in world politice. As already mentioned, the normalization of relations with the Soviet Union began after the Shah's pledge to Moscow, prohibiting foreign missile bases in Iran. Iran's trade and economic and technical relations with the Soviet Union improved significantly, as evidenced by the Soviet construction of Iran's first steel mill and the Trans-Iranian Gas Pipeline. In fact, the Soviets were contributing to the success of the Shah's "White Revolution." The American attitude was equally helpful. Now less critical than before, because of preoccupation with the war in Vietnam, and the more permissive stance of the Johnson Administration, the United States sent the Shah's regime the first major post-Kennedy American arms aid in 1964.

The dramatic change in Iran's capacity for international, especially regional, activity, derived primarily from three separate developments: the 1968 announcement of a 1971 British withdrawal from "east of Suez"; the United States' adoption of the Nixon Doctrine with Iran acting as "policeman of the Gulf"; and the mushrooming of oil revenues after the 1973 Arab-Israeli War. First, Britain announced its historic decision in 1968 to withdraw its forces from the area "east of Suez," including the Persian Gulf, by the end of 1971. Its prolonged negotiations with the Shah's regime on the future of the Gulf islands of Abu Musa and the two Tunbs were inconclusive, except for the Shah's controversial agreement with the Sheikh of Sharjeh permitting the landing of Iranian forces on Abu Musa.

The Shah, however, also landed troops on the two Tunbs in defiance of the claim of the Sheikh of Ras al-Khaimah. This move seemed to establish Iranian control of the entrance of the Persian Gulf and the strategic Strait of Hormuz through which oil tankers carried some 57 percent of the world oil trade. Iran justified its move in terms of both historical claims and strategic requirements of the time.

Second, the United States adoption of the Nixon Doctrine in 1969 as applied to the Persian Gulf meant that the most strategically located, the most populous, and the most economically and militarily advanced Gulf state, Iran, was an "ideal of the Nixon Doctrine." Washington's reluctance to act as the British legatee made this seem all the more plausible, although some spoke of a so-called "twin-pillar" policy, meaning that the Gulf security and stability should be protected by Saudi Arabia as well as Iran. Britain and the United States underwrote the Shah's ambition of acting as the Gulf "policeman" by aiding Iran's military buildup to an unprecedented extent. American support of the Shah's determination to create a "credible deterrent" in the region was crowned in May 1972 by President Nixon's assurances to sell Iran sophisticated American weapons. To be sure, the indiscriminate application of these assurances was a major cause of Iran's subsequent massive, wasteful and expensive arms purchases. By themselves, however, they would not have had such grave consequences. The extravagance of later purchases was helped by the explosion of Iran's oil revenues.

Third, following the Arab-Israeli war of October 1973 Iran's oil revenues increased from a mere $194 million in 1972 to about $22 billion in 1974. The Shah's dream of a "Great Civilization" appeared to be suddenly at hand. Economically he wished to transform Iran into an industrialized state equal to Britain and West Germany in a matter of years; militarily he aspired to change Iran to one of the world's five major non-nuclear powers. Thus, Iran's military expenditures surpassed those of the most powerful Indian Ocean states, including Australia, Indonesia, Pakistan, South Africa and India. The Shah also planned to spend an estimated $33 billion (some experts say three times as much) for the construction of twenty nuclear reactors by 1994. If constructed with German, French, and American aid, they would have made Iran the largest producer of nuclear energy in the entire Indian Ocean area.

The spectular rise in oil revenues during 1974 and what the Shah's regime did with them domestically and internationally was a "disaster in disguise." Domestically, the wasteful and grandiose economic projects, the ever-increasing maldistribution of wealth, the widespread corruption, the over-heating of the economy and myriad other problems destroyed the relative balance between the material benefits of modernization and the social, psychological and cultural costs, a balance that had been maintained somewhat during the mid-1960s. Furthermore, the excesses of political suppression reached a new height after 1974. The creation of the *Rastakhiz* Party and the destruction of the facade of a two-party system in 1975 symbolized the height of political intolerance. Even after the launching of the so-called program of "political liberalization" and fruitless talks about revamping the single-party system in 1978, no real efforts were made to accommodate the forces of political opposition, even the moderate ones. As late as August 5, 1978, for example, the Shah tarred the moderate Nationalist

Frontists and the communists with the same brush. The elements of the religious opposition were characterized as "Islamic Marxist." The Shah's attempt at political liberalization at this time, as in 1961-63, was primarily a token gesture for Washington to ensure support for his regime.

The Shah's foreign policy also contributed to the "revolution of rising alienation." He characterized his foreign policy as "independent" policy, a label actually borrowed from the opposition groups in the early 1960s. As a matter of fact he did attempt to deal with the superpowers pragmatically; and despite his alliance with the United States, he attempted to normalize relations with the Soviet Union. His subsequent regional policies in the Persian Gulf and adjacent areas of the Middle East, South Asia, and the Horn of Africa, however, intensified tensions between Teheran and Moscow and simutaneously deepened the Shah's reliance on the United States, particularly after 1974. The opposition, of course, perceived that American-Iranian "special relationship" in a very negative light. Tudeh members and sympathizers on the left saw it from their historical pro-Soviet and anti-American ideological standpoint. The National Front centrists saw it against the background of American aid to the destruction of the Musaddiq government in 1953. Religious fundamentalists viewed it against the backdrop of the bloody suppression of the Qum uprising in 1963 and the exile of Khomeini in 1964. All believed that the Shah's foreign policy had made Iran utterly subservient to Washington.

IX. (1978-1979) *The Sixth Crisis of the Century: The Shah's Departure and the Evolving Transition*

The Shah lost control of the government in the final months of 1978. In the face of tremendous pressures from both inside and outside Iran, the Shah left his country in mid-January 1979.

The seizure of power by revolutionary forces on February 11, 1979, was followed by the inability of their leaders to consolidate power swiftly. As a result, power and authority were dispersed among a multitude of forces. Then Prime Minister Mehdi Bazargan aptly characterized the crisis as a situation with a "thousand chiefs." The question at this point is whether the sixth Iranian crisis is different from the five preceeding ones. Some argue that it is quite unlike any other crisis in Iran's modern political history because: it destroyed rather than supplemented the monarchy and severed its traditional ties with the armed forces; it had the most widespread base of popular support; it involved more cost in human life and material wealth than the sum total of all previous twentieth-century crises; and it produced more far-reaching international repercussions than all previous crises. Yet, the current crisis has a number of features in common with its precursors. One is especially relevant: That the fundamental problem is the **establishment of an effective governmental authority in Iran**. Today as before, this remains the one condition that will most influence the government's ability to cope with a multitude of economic, social, constitutional and other problems besetting the entire political system.

The first obstacle to the establishment of governmental authority was the transfer of real power from Ayatollah Khomeini and his religious entourage to the provisional government under Prime Minister Bazargan.

Contrary to his own and others' expectations Khomeini was not able to confine his role to "spiritual" guadance in government. He has in fact acted as the defacto head of state.

Iran's capacity to act effectively in foreign affairs will depend not only on the transfer of power from the Khomeini groups to the government, but on the government's ability to centralize and unify the disparate armed forces. This basic problem has three related aspects. First the reconstruction of the armed forces should be a most difficult problem for the government. The seizure of power in February 1979 by the revolutionary forces in Teheran severed, for the first time, the traditional alliance between the monarch and the military. The Shah's hated SAVAK had been disestablished by the revolutionary forces. The 413,000-man armed forces, however, had been paralyzed and demoralized since then, despite reports to the effect that the basic structures have remained "intact" in varying degrees in the Army, Navy and Air Force. A subsequent purge, mass dismissal of high-ranking officers, and executions have further added to the problems of military reconstruction. Second, the government must disarm a multitude of motley forces that captured arms in the chaotic conditions surrounding the seizure of power from the military. The third aspect of the problem is the competition of various groups with both the government and the Khomeini followers. The government believes that the armed forces have already been sufficiently "purified" and should be reconstructed. While the armed forces have been informally under the control of the government, Khomeini followers and other groups have already penetrated the military and probably are competing for its control.

Initially, in addition to the Bazargan government and Khomeini revolutionary committees, two major groups in particular competed for control of the armed forces. The largest group was the Islamic "People's Mujahedin of Iran." This group generally has followed the Khomeini line, but is quite independent and lies to the left of the Ayatollah. The Mujahedin earlier placed itself under the general supervision of Ayatollah Taleqani, who had been a founder of the National Front, although not formally a Front leader. The Mujahedin did recruit some members of the armed forces and competed for the control of the Army's lower ranks. The Marxist "People's Fedayeen of Iran" has also sought influence in the armed forces and has called for radical changes, such as the creation of a "People's Army" run by soldier committees and elected officers.

Khomeini, however, did not seem to believe that infiltration of the armed forces by armed elements of his revolutionary committees were sufficient for protecting the revolution. He subsequently created the Revolutionary Guards. The Bazargan government had believed that the Guards should obey its orders, but actually the the 6,000-man force had been placed under the direct control of the secret Council and was headed by one of Khomeini's closest associates, Ayatollah Lahuti. According to its formal charter, the aim of the Revolutionary Guards is "to protect the revolution in Iran and to spread it in the world in keeping with genuine Islamic principles." The stated responsibilities of the Guards include aiding the maintenance of internal security; combatting counterrevolutionary activities; implementing the orders of the revolutionary courts; defending against foreign aggression; providing "moral, ideological, and military training for army officers"; and supporting "just liberation movements of the down-trodden masses of the world under the leadership of the revolution and in consultation with the government."

Relations With the United States

Iran's relations with the United States have undergone revolutionary change since the downfall of the Shah's regime. The reliance of the Shah on the United States, dating back to World War II and especially to the fall of Musaddiq in 1953, skyrocketed after the British departure from the Persian Gulf and the fourfold rise of oil revenues in 1973-74. This reliance identified the United States government with all that the Shah did, or failed to do, in the eyes of the opposition. While this legacy of association between the United States and the Shah's regime is itself an influential factor in the attitudes and policies of the revolutionary regime, it became reinforced by ideological influences.

One of the most powerful ideological influences is based on a particular Shi'i Muslim interpretation of the contemporary world. To be sure, this interpretation is used by some elements of the conservative religious leaders to rationalize their quest for power, but it would be a mistake to leave it at that. There are other religious leaders, including Khomeini himself, who probably see the world through that ideological perspective. They are sincere believers, and we must take them at their word.

Briefly stated, this particular interpretation starts with a specific verse in the Koran. It was first used by Khomeini and has ever since been invoked by his associates in expounding the Islamic ideological basis of their attitudes and actions, ranging from summary trials and executions by the revolutionary courts to the views of revolutionary leaders on world politics. Khomeini's Koranic inspired sentence is : "The down—trodden must truimph over the dominant elements" (bayed mostazafin bar mostakberin ghalabeh konand). The translation is, of course, inadequate for understanding the two key concepts of "mostazafin" and "mostakberin." The first concept is not confined to those who are simply "impoverished" since this usual, but wrong, rendition in English connotes those who are economically downtrodden. According to Shi'i interpretation, the concept includes those who are not only exploited economically, but also mistreated socially, deprived culturally or oppressed politically. The second concept is also open-ended. It means those who are "dominant," not only economically, but also socially, culturally, or politically. Furthermore, the two concepts are stretched to include not only groups and individuals, but also states and governments in world politics.

From such a perspective, the masses in Iran were domestically "downtrodden" while the deposed Shah, former Prime Minister Abbas Hoveyda and other former high-ranking civilian and military officials were viewed as the "dominant" elements. The summary trials and executions fulfilled Khomeini's Koran-based call for the triumph of the "downtrodden elements. At the international level, the superpowers, large cartels, trusts, multinational corporations and in a work "capitalist imperialism and socialist imperialism" constitute the "dominant elements" as to their "Zionist, Phalangist and Fascist" instruments. In this context the fundamental goal of the Koran is the creation of a "united people" (ummat-e vehedeh) where all the problems associated with dichotomy and imbalance between dominant and downtrodden elements will disappear in a justice and equality-oriented Islamic order. This account is based on the view of an unknown member of Khomeini's Revolutionary Council, but is also a perspective that is probably shared by many of his associates.[2] It is also a perspective that is reflected in the so-called "theories" of Dr. Abol-Hassan Banisadr, the lay radical economist regarded by his sympathizers as the

"Islamic thinker" (mutefakker-e Islami) of the revolutionary regime. He theorizes, for example, that during the last 25 years of the Shah's rule Iran was rapidly integrated into the world economy by means of the export of oil and import of goods produced by the industrial nations. As a result Iran became "ever more a tributary of foreign economies."[3] Those who divided Iran's oil revenues constituted the dominant classes, and they in turn were "in reality only the agents" for the world dominant or hegemonic classes of the West and the multinational corporations. Thus real emancipation of Iran required the emasculation of the country's dependency relationship with the West and the multinational firms. Ever since the seizure of power by the revolutionary forces, Banisadr has repeatedly called for the nationalization of banks and insurnace companies, and has expounded his radical views in books, articles and many lectures.

The identification of the United States with the Shah's regime and the ideological stance of Khomeini and his close aides are not the only factors influencing Iran's attitude toward the United States. In his angry denunciation of the Senate resolution condemning executions in Iran, Khomeini categorically stated, "We have no need for the United States; it is they who need us as a source of oil, for which their greed never ceases."[4] The anti-American, anti-Western attitude of the Ayatollah surfaced repeatedly in his charges of complicity of American agents in the assassination of Ayatollah Motahhari and the attempt against the like of Ayatollah Rafsanjani. There is little doubt that many of his vitriolic charges against the United States are for domestic consumption, especially trying to beat the leftist groups at their anti-American game. Radical statements also are a reflection of the unsettled revolutionary situation in Iran. Yet these considerations should not be exaggerated. Anti-Americanism, ideological influences and a limited view of American utility to the revolutionary regime are real factors.

There are a number of constraints on the regime's attitude toward the United States. One is the very existence of the more moderate technocratic and modern-educated elements in Iran. Another constraint is the age-old strategic predicament of Iran. Khomeini is fiercely anti-communist and anti-Soviet. Furthermore, historically no Iranian government has ever been able to ignore the Russian problem; it is a geopolitical reality. A third constraint on the revolutionary regime's anti-American attitude is a deep concern with the perceived atheistic leftist groups, whether the Marxist Fedayeen or the revived Tudeh communist party. Finally, the revolutionary regime will have to cope urgently with mounting economic and security problems both inherited from the Shah's regime and produced by the ongoing revolutionary crisis. Iran could use American markets for its oil exports, military and economic know-how for security and development, and spare parts and capital goods.

Relations With the Soviet Union

The prospects of the revolutionary regime's relations with the Soviet Union would appear to be bright. First, pronouncements by the Khomeini group regarding the Soviet Union while occasionally associating it with Western countries, Zionists, and Israel have hardly resembled the repeated vitriolic denunciations of American imperialism. Khomeini himself has characterized the United States as "the principal enemy" (doshman-e asli). Second, the fall of the Shah's regime and the demise of his long-standing alliance and extensive economic relations with the United States would appear to be a definite gain for the Soviets. Their goal of undermining CENTO has already been achieved. Furthermore, another Soviet goal, that of undermining the Western consortium of oil companies' operation in Iran, has also been realized. Third, the regional attitudes and policies of the revolutionary regime all would seem to coincide with the Soviet position, as Moscow has gleefully acknowledged. The rupture of diplomatic relations with Israel; the embracement of the PLO; the disengagement from Oman and the general reversal of the Shah's Persian Gulf policy, which was opposed by Moscow from the beginning; the rupture of diplomatic relations with Egypt; the establishment of contacts with South Yemen and Libya; and the withdrawal of Iran's support for American peace-making efforts in the Middle East would all appear to show the coincidence of Soviet and Iranian interests. On the Basis of these and similar considerations it would be easy therefore to conclude that the revolutionary regime's relations with the Soviet Union are likely to improve and might even tilt favorably toward Moscow.

Yet, there are equally strong indications to the contrary. First the revolutionary leadership has remained highly suspicious of the Soviet Union despite its less frequent denunciation of Moscow. The Soviet Union has enjoyed no position in Iran comparable to that of the United States since World War II. On the contrary, over the half century of the Pahlavi dynasty or the one and a half centuries from the Russian imposition of the Treaty of Turkomanchai (1828) to the downfall of the Shah's regime, Iran as a state often had bitter experiences and limited relations with Russia. This has been an aspect of what I call Iran's "diplomatic culture" that Ayatollah Khomeini has not been, and is not likely to be, able to escape. To be sure, Iran already has an Ambassador in Moscow (Mohammad Mokry); the Soviets have an envoy in Teheran (Vladimir M. Vinogradov), the first to be received by the Ayatollah Khomeini.

But what did all this amount to? Khomeini told the Soviet Ambassador, for example: "This is an Islamic Government under the supervision of Islamic leaders."[5] According to his spokesman he added that Iran would defend its independence and territorial integrity against any power and asked all foreign powers "not to interfere in our domestic affairs." More interestingly he spoke to the Ambassador about Iran's future economic and commercial relations only. These were the only real relations developed with Moscow before the revolution. Even these limited relations would be conducted, he said, "only with Iran's interests in mind." Suspicion of the Soviets surfaced even more clearly during the Kurdish uprisings, when Ahmad Sadr, Minister of Interior, told newsmen that "that Soviet Union pretends to be a friendly country, but we are quite aware that they are trying to cause troubles with agents."[6] He thought Moscow was helping to exploit Iran's age-old security problems with the Turkomans and Baluchi, Kurdish, and Arab minorities.

Second, the revolutionary leadership's hostile attitude toward communism is more than an expression of Islamic fundamentalism. It is also an expression of Iran's concrete experience with the communist Tudeh Party. In the Iranian political culture this party generally is considered a "political leper." Deep distrust of the party grew out of its perceived subservience to Moscow. The party has been revived, and its Secretary General, Nouredin Kianuri, returned to Iran after twenty-five years spent in exile mostly in the Soviet Union and Eastern Europe. Tudeh leaders consider their party legal in defiance of the negative attitude of the government. Form Moscow's perspective Kianouri's return, his party's open activities, and the publication and open dissemination of the Tudeh official paper, *Mardum* (People), for the first time in 37 years have pointed to a significant and potential target of Soviet opportunity of Iran.

Most Iranian groups, including the Marxist Fedayeen, keep their distance from the Tudeh Party. From its revival after the abdication of Reza Shah in 1941 until its effective suppression in 1954 and again a decade later, on more than one occasion the party revealed its real nature: it sang the tune of Moscow unabashedly in the 1944 oil concession crisis, in the 1945-46 Azerbaijan crisis, and in the 1951-1953 oil nationalization crisis, when it prematurely celebrated the establishment of the "People's Republic of Iran" with the complete approval of Moscow.

Third, the revolutionary regime's crusade for Islam should concern the Soviets in the future as it has already. In this respect the Ayatollah Shariatmadari, who holds no official position, but who enjoys emmense popularity in the Soviet-Iranian border province of Azerbaijan, has been quite outspoken. The Ayatollah, for example, told the correspondents of *Pravda, Izvestia,* and *Tass* in Teheran that the Soviet Union must accord greater freedom to its own forty-five million Muslims, and should not allow the pro-Soviet government of Afghanistan to suppress Afghani religious leaders and intellectuals. Although the interview was not published in Moscow, it was printed in the Iranian newspapers with jubilation. The problem of Islamic-inspired political "contagion," according to Fred Coleman of *Newsweek*, a visitor to Muslim areas in the Soviet Union, is best exemplified in Baku, an oil center on the Caspian Sea which abuts Iran and the Soviet Union. The 1.5 million Muslims of the capital city of Soviet Azerbaijan Republic have the closest link to the Muslim protest movement that swept the revolutionary forces to power in Iran.

Finally, the future relations of the revolutionary regime with Moscow should continue to be adversely affected by differences over concrete issues in their economic and commercial transactions as they were prior to the revolution. The Shah's regime not only constructed the Trans-Iranian Gas Pipeline to the Soviet Union, but was seriously considering the building of an additional $2.5 pipeline designed to carry natural gas to the Soviet Union for distribution to West Germany, Austria, Italy and Czechoslovakia in return for 17 billion cubic meters of Iranian supplies a year piped to the Soviet Union's southern republics. It appeared almost certain in May 1979 that the revolutionary regime would cancel the plan. Many Iranians have criticized the Trans-Iranian Gas Pipeline and have demanded that Iranian natural gas be kept for domestic consumption. The reduced level of oil production by the revolutionary regime has not only made the world oil market tight and more expensive for the West, but also has resulted in curtailed gas deliveries to the Soviet Union and has forced the Soviets to make costly redistributions of energy supplies for industries in the Transcaucasian region. Moreover, the price of Iranian natural gas piped to the Soviet Union has been disputed by the new regime as it was prior to the revolution.

Conclusions

On the basis of the foregoing discussions what are the principal propositions that may be suggestive in thinking about Iran's capacity for action in world politics in crisis situations? More particularly, how' does Iran's capacity in the current revolution compare with the previous major crises? And, more importantly, what are the salient lessons of the Iranian situation for American policy toward Iran and the closely related issues in the Persian Gulf and the Middle East.?

In all the major crises of the past the crucial variables were two: the degree of consolidation of domestic political power and the nature and extent of foreign intervention. The first variable would include such major problems as territorial integrity, functioning economy, proliferation and polarization of political forces and political participation and institutionalization. The second variable would refer to foreign intervention in support of, or in opposition to, the central government.

As contrasted with most previous crises, Iran's capacity for action in world politics is likely to be greater in the current revolution. It is likely to be greater than in the first crisis (1905-14) because the degree of domestic consolidation of power would be relatively higher and the extent of adverse foreign intervention relatively lower. Recall the combination of nearly total breakdown of governmental authority and repeated adverse British and Russian military intervention and political interference against the Constitutional regime. As contrasted with the second crisis (1914-51), again the same proposition would generally hold true. Recall frequent government crises throughout the World War and in its aftermath, despite the governments of a few skillful Prime Ministers (Foroughi, Sa'ed and Qavam.) (Razmara was strong, but his term was too short). Insofar as adverse foreign intervention and interference are concerned, remember the international problem of Soviet reluctance to withdraw the Red Army troops from Iran and Soviet support for separatist regimes in Azerbaijan and Kurdistan

The ability of this revolutionary regime in foreign affairs is likely to be greater than that of Musaddiq (1951-53), because of the same basic considerations. Musaddiq's authority crisis was, as seen, compounded by the combined British and American opposition to his government. Even if the consolidation of power in the current revolutionary crisis should surn out to be as serious, the problem of foreign intervention might not arise.* Despite all Iranian charges of intervention by the superpowers, particularly the United States, the current revolutionary regime faces no threat of great power intervention comparable to that in all previous crises of the twentieth century.

Yet the external environment facing the revolutionary regime might change dramatically. Recall the change in American policy toward the Musaddiq government from an impartial, if not supportive, role to one of opposition. The primary reason for that change of attitude was the rear of a communist coup in Iran. That fear is by no means absent today, but the main concern of the United States is to secure access to Persian Gulf oil supplies in adequate amounts and at equitable prices now and in the near future. The Iranian revolution has intensified that basic concern which is shared significantly by other Western industrialized societies, Japan and numerous oil-poor developing states that are more dependent on Gulf oil

---

*About fifteen months after this article had been written, Iraq invaded Iran on 22 September 1980.

than the United States. That basic concern undergirds a potential reversal of American post-Vietnam hands-off policy in the Persian Gulf, as evidenced by talks about U.S. military intervention in the event of adverse circumstances threatening the flow of Gulf oil supplies to world markets. Adverse circumstances could arise from any source, ranging from local conflicts and Soviet covert or overt intervention, to domestic turmoil.

The salient lessons of the Iranian revolution for American Gulf policy in general and U.S. policy toward Iran in particular point out what would seem to be the advantages and disadvantages of Defense Secretary Harold Brown's formula for Middle East security and suggest, alternatively, a new concept of security.[7] That concept would require American determination to cooperate with the Gulf states in their efforts to maintain regional security, but the United States should include the OECD countries in such an approach rather than engage in a solo performance. The basic idea involved is twofold: First, U.S. vital interests would be better served by taking into account authentic regional and internal developments in the Gulf and the Middle East and the needs and sensitivities of our Western allies and friends. Second, those interests would be better protected by avoiding any compensation for excessive U.S. reticence of yesterday by umbridled intervention tomorrow. The latter posture would be perceived as an attempt to turn the Gulf into an American lake, just as the Shah's position was perceived as aiming at transforming it into a Persian lake. The latter did, the former would, run afoul of the region's cultural, social, political and economic values and interests as a whole.

In every previous crisis of the twentieth century in Iran the external environment had a profound effect on the outcome of the cirsis. In the recent crisis, our indecisiveness might have had as much to do with the Shah's downfall on the Carter Administration (as Henry Kissinger seems to do), as to attribute it to the Kissinger-Nixon decision of 1972 to sell the Shah whatever arms he wanted (as George Ball seems to suggest). Our basic failure dates back to 1953 when the United States helped to return the Shah to power without realizing that his imposed tranquility in Iran would be no substitute for genuine social and economic development and most particularly for real efforts toward the institutionalization of political change and participation. When the Shah took the throne in 1941, the British and the Russians endorsed his government contingent on his respect for the constitution of Iran. No such assurance was sought or granted in 1953.

Perhaps the single most important lesson of the Iranian experience is that jmposed tranquility is a substitute for neither genuine political stability nor real regional security. Iran's international capacity increased perceptibly during three periods of imposed tranquility under two authoritarian Shahs (1921-41; 1953-63; 1964-78). For Iranians today, however, the fundamental question is whether Iran can escape, for the first time in history, still another return to domestic authoritarian tranquility and a new facade of external capability. For the United States, the Iranian experience raises an equally important question. Can the United States develop, for the first time since World War II, a new concept of stability for the Middle East that would transcent the traditional confines of preserving the status quo in an era and area of unprecedented social, economic, political and foreign policy change?[8] So far the American reaction to the far-reaching impact of the Iranian revolution would seem to have found primary expression in the search for military solutions to an extremely complex situation. The post-Shah Middle East situation would seem to demand first and foremost constructive and comprehensive economic, political and diplomatic initiative. The need for a comprehensive economic, political and diplomatic initiatives. The need for a comprehensive American conception of the Middle East situation became abundantly clear after the Arab-Israeli war of October 1973.[9] Today's increased need for contingency plans for military initiatives must not be allowed to becloud the fact that the post-Shah situation in the Middle East poses multifaceted, interlocking, region-wide challenges to American foreign policy. They would require not only a new conception, but also an imaginative strategy that would call for the employment of a wide range of economic, political, diplomatic, and cultural means. There are times in the relations of states when force must be used in defense of vital interests, and there is no substitute for it. Military means, however, must complement these other means only under extremely adverse circumstances.

NOTES

1. See Fred Halliday, *Iran: Dictatorship and Development* (Middlesex, England: Penguin Books Ltd., 1979), p. 138
2. For details see *Ettala'at* (in Persian), No. 15826, 10 April 1979.
3. See Abdol-Hassan Banisadr and Paul Vieille, "Iran and the Multinationals," in Ali-Reza Nobari, ed., *Iran Erupts* (Stanford: the Iran-America Development Group, 1978), pp. 24-33. The most complete views of Banisadr, however, are to be found in Persian, especially in his *Naft va Sulteh ya Naqsh-e Naft dar Pahnehye Jahan va Zaman* (presumably, Tehran: Entesharat Mosaddiq, 1977).
4. *New York Times*, 21 May 1979.
5. See *New York Times*, 26 February 1979. On 12 June 1979 in an unusally sharp exchange with the Soviet Ambassador, Khomeini charged that the Soviet Union was possibly interferring in Iran, see *New York Times*, 13 June 1979.
6. See *Washington Post*, Rowland Evans and Robert Norvak, 9 April 1979.
7. See Rouhollah K. Ramazani, "Security in the Persian Gulf," *Foreign Affairs*, 57 (Spring 1979), pp. 821-835.
8. As early as 1964 I pointed out the need for such a new concept; it is all the more needed now. See Rouhollah K. Ramazani, "Changing United States Policy in the Middle East," *Virginia Quarterly Review*, 40, No. 3 (1964), pp. 369-382.
9. This was fully and critically pointed out in Rouhollah K. Ramazani, *Beyond the Arab-Israeli Settlement: New Directions for U.S. Policy in the Middle East* (Cambridge, Massachusetts: Institute for Foreign Policy Analysis, Inc., 1977).

II. THE IRANIAN REVOLUTION OF 1978-79: POTENTIAL IMPLICATIONS FOR MAJOR COUNTRIES IN THE AREA

Robert Ghobad Darius

The ultimate objective of the 1978-79 revolution in Iran is to transform its political system. The revolution in Iran was massive, broad-based and supported by most of the Iranian people.[1] It represented a zenith in Iran's contemporary history and lacks significant parallels in Western, bourgeois models of revolution. The Iranian revolution was indigenous, deeply-rooted in Iran's cultural, religious, foreign policy, developmental aspirations and changing identity. It would be premature and superficial to generalize about the Iranian revolution in the framework of Western stereotypes and models.

The Iranian revolution reflects Iranian nationalism and the prolonged historic struggle between the two Pahlavi shahs and Iran's religious population and growing middle class. In this context, the simplified, often politicized debate in the United States over who "lost" Iran failed to reflect the deep roots of the upheavals. Traditions and values as deeply rooted as those in Iran die hard. In Mohammad Reza Shah Pahlavi's dictatorial system, which was dedicated to the change of traditional nationally-held values, and with the Shah's powerful and much feared secret service (SAVAK), which aroused popular hatred, traditional values and institutions were revived and reawakened to threaten the basic pre-

---

The views, opinions, and/or findings contained in this report are those of the author and should not be construed as an official Department of the Army position, policy or decision, unless so designated by other official documentation.

mise of legitimacy of the Pahlavi dynasty on a scale unprecedented in contemporary Iranian history. This threat to the Shah was unparalleled for its ". . . discipline in the face of Government violence. As such, it will long be studied for its lessons in agitational politics and mass organization."[2]

Iran's "unexpected" revolution suprised not only the U.S. leaders and other foreign leaders, but also the Shah of Iran himself and his confidants. The Shah and his top aides relied on SAVAK for information on domestic dissidents. SAVAK consistently underestimated the extent of the growing opposition to the Shah. U.S. intelligence also relied heavily on SAVAK for information on domestic Iranian affairs, and as a result, also failed to estimate and analyze accurately the developing situation. Moreover, in Iran, most Americans did not establish or maintain contacts with the leaders of groups in opposition to the Shah. Americans in Iran socialized mainly with other Americans and with wealthy, Western-educated pro-Shah Iranians. As a result, they failed to understand the ground swell of opposition against the Shah.

In the U.S. academic community, some scholars, such as Richard Cottam and Hamid Algar, warned their readers of the deep malaise in Iran's political system; the necessity to reevaluate U.S. foreign policy toward Iran; and the need to understand the deeply ingrained Shia religious roots against dictatorship and tyranny. Other scholars, such as Professor Leonard Binder, wrote as late as January 1979 that "it is apparent that the government of the Shah is responding quite skillfully to the crisis. We would be misled if we underestimated the resources at the disposal of the Shah. . . ." Binder maintained that thus far the middle class was "outmanoeuvered and overpowered by the monarchy."[3] Professor Hamid Algar stated prior to the Iranian Revolution of 1978-79 that the opposition to tyranny was "one of the fundamental and most pervasive characteristics" of Shia Islam.[4] In Algar's opinion, there was a definite linkage between the role played by the *ulamas* (theologians), as the major opposition force against the Qajar dynasty in Iran's Constitutional Revolution of 1905-1911, and the struggle by the *ulamas* against the Pahlavi dynasty in the present period. The *ulamas* in both periods were opposed to tyranny and dictatorship. Algar's profound analyses introduce the reader to the historic and religious factors which contributed to the 1978-79 upheavals in Iran.

This paper focuses on the Iranian Revolution of 1978-79, its roots, its major domestic and external actors, the factors that led to the eruption of the upheavals in 1978, the options to consolidate the Iranian revolution and some of the potential implications of the revolution for major countries in the area.

THE ROOTS OF THE IRANIAN REVOLUTION

The political roots of the Iranian revolution can, at least, be traced to the Iranian Constitutional Revolution of 1905-1911, which was essentially led by the *ulamas* to reduce the absolute, arbitrary power of the Qajar dynasty. The attitudes and views of Iranians are deeply and unalterably influenced by the political philosophy of Prophet Ali; the martyrdom of Shia Islamic leaders; the continuing theme in Shia Islam of the need for justice; and the legitimacy of the ruler.

Legitimate rule is one of the most critical tests of a leader's survival. Lack of popular support and legitimacy were the principal factors which contributed to the downfall of the Shah. Legitimate rule, according to the political theory of *Ithna ashari* Shia Islam, belongs to the *Imam* alone. There are only 12 *Imams* in Shia Islam. The Twelfth *Imam*, Mohammad al-Mahdi's occultation in 847 A.D., ended in the disappearance of even the possibility of legitimacy of rule.[5] As a result, Iran's Shia national regimes and leaders have been viewed as repugnant usurpers, an ingrained attitude which prevailed in Iran throughout both the Qajar and the Pahlavi dynasties. Rulers in Shia Islam appear to be far more vulnerable to such popular political and religious attitudes of their people than rulers in Sunni Islamic lands.

The quest for social justice and a general repugnance toward tyranny are two critical underpinnings of socialization in Iran's Shia political culture.[6] As a rule, popular attitudes and aspirations play a vital role in Iran in denying legitimacy to anyone who rules arbitrarily. The Shah's arbitrary, dictatorial methods, and the brutality of his SAVAK, resulted in a latent, permanent freeze on legitimacy of his regime. The Shah, as the ruler and the symbol of authority ignored these deeply ingrained popular attitudes and aspirations. His dictatorial methods increased popular disaffection and repugnance toward him and his rule and ultimately led to his ouster from power.

During the Pahlavi dynasty (1925-1978), massive modernization and secularization efforts were undertaken in Iran. These efforts to modernize Iran were successful, but they weakened traditional Islamic Shia leadership and institutions, and reduced the power and the self-esteem of the Shia *ulamas*. The modernization effort resulted in a politico-religious backlash by Iran's 32 million religious Shia Moslems to whom secularization and modernization, directed from above, without popular consent, were viewed as another clear manifestation of arbitrary decisionmaking by the Shah. In this contest, the Iranian upheavals were, in part, a consequence of rapid industrialization, arbitrary decisionmaking by the Shah, rising expectations at all levels of society, frustration of those expectations, the failure on the part of the Shah to seek popular consensus for his plans, and to lead the nation in a manner consistent with its traditional values. In its anatomy, the Iranian revolution appears to establish a precedent for some of the basic aspects of the pattern of revolutions particularly for the underdeveloped Moslem countries around the world; deeply ingrained traditional politico-religious values are threatened by a massive modernization; rising expectations are frustrated; catalytic events radicalize the population; forces of nationalism are misperceived; and charismatic leader overthrows an established regime which lacks popular support and legitimacy.

Finally, the Shah neglected, misunderstood, and underestimated the forces of Iranian nationalism which were unleashed by Dr. Mohammad Mossadegh and his supporters in the 1950-53 period. This was the first manifestation of Iranian nationalism in the post-World War II era; Mossadegh's popularity in Iran was unassailable and his personal standing was extremely high among Iranian nationalists. According to Richard Cottam, Mossadegh's "atavistic view of British influence in Iran and the Middle East prevented him from understanding that the battle had been won when the British accepted the principle of nationalization of oil"[7] Iranian nationalism of the Mossadegh era "floundered on the shoals of its own irrationality . . . Mossadegh was as much a prisoner of the irrationality as were many of his least literate supporters." The Shah, instead of grasping the significance of nationalism as a potent force, created obstacles in its path in Iran, further strengthening the basis of support for nationalism and eroding his own sources of legitimacy.

Since its inception, the Pahlavi dynasty failed to deal successfully with serious socio-economic problems facing Iran. These problems festered for decades, perpetuating popular discontent with the Shah. Furthermore, many Iranians resented the extent and degree of corruption in their country. They believed high-level corruption which blocked benefits for the masses must be ended; however, in their opinion, it was impossible to end wide-scale corruption as long as the members of the Pahlavi family were themselves deeply involved in wide-scale corruption. The next section focuses on some of the major domestic and external actors in the Iranian upheavals.

MAJOR DOMESTIC AND EXTERNAL ACTORS

The major domestic and external actors and participants in the Iranian revolution of 1978-79 and an account of their sources of support and opposition are as follows:

(a) Mohammad Reza Shah Pahlavi had the support of the modern and well-armed Imperial Iranian Armed Forces. With their support, he felt secure and could not foresee that the Pahlavi dynasty would be seriously threatened by an internal element, as long as SAVAK succeeded in keeping the populace under control. As long as there was stability, the wealthy upper class appeared to support the Shah, as did most of the bureaucrats, some of the lower middle class, Iran's tribal population, and most of its minorities (Assyrians, Bahais, Baluchis, Jews, Kurds, and Zoroastrians). The Shah and the government of Iran also appeared to be widely supported abroad.

(b) Ayatollah Rouhallah Khomeini, the 78-year-old symbol of opposition to the Pahlavi dynasty, had suffered personally during the reign of the Pahlavis. His father was killed in the early part of this century, and his son was killed by SAVAK in the mid 1970's. Khomeini is the most important of the approximately 12 prominent ayatollahs in Iran. There are some 350 ayatollahs in Iran and approximately 1200 in the Islamic world. Due to his impeccable reputation for honesty and longstanding opposition to the Shah, Ayatollah Khomeini became extremely popular with the masses of Iranians. During his 15 years in exile, Ayatollah Khomeini, in the perception of most Iranians, became the national symbol of resistance. Other ayatollahs, *ulamas,* and mullahs acting under the direction of Ayatollah Khomeini formed the religious organizational nucleus for the forces opposing the Shah. Shahriar Rouhani, the young intellectual in charge of Iranian interests in the United States during the early phase of the revolution, has summarized the perception of the Iranian people toward Ayatollah Khomeini as follows:

> The people of Iran are struggling for survival as a nation. Khomeini is the symbol and rallying point of this struggle. . . The people look at Khomeini for leadership and there is no alternative to his charisma. Instead of heading the state as a charismatic leader, which could result in a possible totalitar-

ianism, he is providing only the general moral direction.[9]

(c) About 32 million of Iran's 36 million population are Shia Moslems. As the Shah pushed his massive modernization efforts, he underestimated the pervasive powers of religion and tradition and neglected to evaluate the disruptive impacts of his efforts on traditional institutions and value systems.

(d) The *Mujahedeen Khalgh*, the major Moslem revolutionary faction supporting Ayatollah Khomeini, received considerable training and assistance from Yasir Arafat's Al Fatah group of the Palestine Liberation Organization (the PLO). The *Mujahedeen Khalgh* played a vital role--particularly after the Shah left Iran--in the Iranian revolution.

(e) The National Coalition Front (NCF) was formed in 1950, as a result of the union of four political parties represented in the Iranian Parliament immediately before the Premiership of Dr. Mohammad Mossadegh. Mossadegh was appointed by the Shah as Iran's premier in 1951, and he became the leader of the NCF. The return of the Shah to power in 1953 marked the suppression of the NCF, and many of its prominent leaders were jailed or exiled. The NCF was reestablished in the 1962-63 period; however, it was once again suppressed by the Shah, and its principal leaders were imprisoned. In December 1977, Karim Sanjabi, Darioush Forouhar, and Shahpour Bakhtiar, all of whom had served as ministers under Dr. Mossadegh, announced the reformation of the NCF, and by August 1978 the NCF included several parties, representing a broad-based coalition of political parties with a specific program designed to restore civil liberties in Iran. The NCF has the support of the middle class, which constitutes about 25 percent of Iran's population.

(f) It is possible that U.S. enunciation of its human rights policy may have encouraged the Shah to expedite his liberalization policy, which in turn contributed to the eruption of the Iranian upheavals. There is a perception that the U.S. human rights policy affected the Shah's response toward the Iranian revolution. The Shah's abrupt and unexpected implementation of a wide-scale liberalization effort in late 1978 was most likely in accordance with Western ideals of human rights, and that policy may have expedited his downfall.

(g) Most Iranian students abroad and many at home were strongly opposed to the Shah. Iranian students in the United States were highly vocal in the 1970's, and they vehemently opposed the Shah after the U.S. human rights policy was announced.

(h) The Marxist *Fedayeen Khalgh* were a small, but effective, element during the revolution. It was well-organized, armed, and it maintained a distance from Moscow. The extent of external support for *Fedayeen Khalgh* remains unclear.

(i) The *Forghan* Fighters, the group that claims responsibility for the killings of General Vali Gharani and Ayatollah Morteza Motahari, played a counter-revolutionary role in a critical period when the consolidation of the revolution was taking place. The *Forghan* Fighters oppose *Akhundha va Akhundbazi*, or rule of *akhunds* and *ulamas* (religious leadership) and institutions. They maintain that *Akhundha* keep people down by superstition and rejection of Westernization, while seeking to acquire power, influence and wealth.[10]

(j) The full extent of Soviet involvement in Iran during the 1978-79 period remains unclear, but it appears that the U.S.S.R. and its friends have and probably will continue to contribute to the upheavals and to the post-revolutionary period.

(k) Yasir Arafat's *Al Fatah* group of the Palestine Liberation Organization (PLO) has been involved in training Iranian Shia Moslem revolutionaries (particularly the *Mujahedeen Khalgh*) for several years. The PLO has supported anti-Shah elements inside and outside Iran, a factor which is shaping one aspect of the foreign policy objectives of the Islamic Republic of Iran.

Crisis and revolutions require a spark. In the Iranian case, an array of factors sparked the upheavals which led to the Iranian revolution. The next section evaluates the principal factors which triggered the revolutionary period in 1978.

THE ERUPTION OF THE IRANIAN REVOLUTION

Due to the dangers of contemporaneity, it is difficult at this time to answer fully the question of why the Iranian Revolution occurred in 1978. As a partial answer to that question, it appears that several factors, unforeseen developments and circumstances provided the needed spark for the severe upheavals in Iran in 1978. Without their joint presence the Iranian monarchy may have temporarily, but not for long, survived a less severe crisis. Among these variables the following are particularly notable:

(a) Most foreign workers, especially Westerners, earned top wages, lived in the best houses available, and enjoyed the highest standard of living in Iran. At the same time, most of the urban Iranians received low wages and suffered from unemployment and an acute shortage of housing, which contributed to their alienation, rebellion, and a rising xenophobia.

(b) After the 1973-74 oil price hikes, spiraling inflation caused severe economic hardships for most Iranians, due to a loss of real earning power. As a result, popular resentment of the Shah, the symbol of authority, increased substantially.

(c) In 1976, due to government attempts to control spiraling inflation, many construction programs in Iran were curtailed significantly. As a result, vast numbers of unskilled workers who had migrated to cities from rural areas to find work in construction and service sectors of the economy were unemployed. This group provided many of the people who participated in the subsequent demonstrations against the Shah.

(d) Rising popular expectations are a sociological phenomenon prevalent throughout the Third World. In Iran, the Pahlavi monarchs through massive exposure to the West helped fuel these rising expectations, but they failed to satisfy them. Instead, a growing and ever-widening gap developed between popular, rising expectations and the capacity and competence of the central government of Iran to meet these demands. The Shah was blamed for the poor performance of the government because he defined himself as the symbol and essence of the nation.

(e) By 1978, the middle class represented about 25 percent of Iran's population. The remarkable increase of Iran's middle class from 1953 to 1978 appears to have been largely ignored by the pro-Shah factions.

(f) The Pahlavis failed to provide adequate political channels for the Iranian people. Disregarding the constitution, both Shahs made decisions in an authoritarian, dictatorial fashion through *Farmans* (Royal Edicts). These edicts were inplemented by loyal, pro-Shah technocrats with little regard for the wishes of the people. This was a prime cause of discontent among the middle class. The Shah created a facade of a political party system, but in reality the parties did not function as in a democratic system, which added to the frustration of Iran's rising middle class.

(g) SAVAK, through its methods of brutality, created an overwhelming atmosphere of distrust, fear, and uncertainty in Iran. The prevailing belief that SAVAK was created by the United States, its personnel trained by Israel, and that it was the brutal instrument of the Shah alienated many Iranians against the Shah and diminished their respect for the United States. Iranians believed that as long as SAVAK existed the people would lack basic human rights.

(h) Most informed Iranians considered the Shah's huge arms expenditures extravagant and unnecessary in light of the immense domestic needs of the people. By placing primary, undue emphasis on foreign policy and defense expenditures, the Shah failed to focus on the basic internal needs of the people.

(i) Ayatollah Rouhallah Khomeini was exiled to Iraq in 1963 and was subsequently forced to leave when Iraq was concerned over relations with the Shah in 1978. As a result, the Ayatollah established a new residence in France, and, with ample access to Western communications, he and his followers substantially expanded their attacks on the Shah. Riots, demonstrations, and rallies against the Shah became routine events both in Iran and abroad. Ayatollah Khomeini's presence to lead the opposition stimulated these events. Strikes in factories and various industries, particularly in the oil sector, were prevalent. These strikes, in conjunction with massive demonstrations in the major cities of Iran, paralyzed Iran's economy, and clearly indicated lack of support for the Shah. As the Shah uncharacteristically made concessions during the earlier phases of the revolution, the opposition began to believe and recognize that their demonstrations, marches, and riots were effective.

(j) The powerful, unexpected alliance between the religious factions and the National Coalition Front substantially expanded the power of the opposition to the Shah. Neither the Shah and his confidants nor most analysts in Iran and abroad predicted that such an effective alliance would take place in 1978. It was the alliance which formed the backbone of the opposition and which posed the greatest single threat to the Shah.

(k) The global Islamic reawakening and reforms had an impact on Iran, and contributed toward the revolution. This reawakening aided the opposition in their efforts to overthrow the Pahlavi dynasty. In short, the country was ripe for a revolution in 1978. The force of events and personalities led to the fulfillment of the revolution earlier than was anticipated.

OPTIONS TO CONSOLIDATE THE IRANIAN REVOLUTION

As long as instability prevails, it would be premature to ignore any conceivable option to consolidate the Iranian revolution. The major options for an eventual consolidation, in an order of priority, include: (1) an Islamic republic; (2) continued instability and unrest; and (3) a people's democratic Islamic republic.

(1) *Islamic republic*

An Islamic republic would be based on the teachings of Islam; the *Sharia,* the laws governing the conduct of man, as set forth in the holy Koran; and *hadith* and *sunna,* interpretations and Islamic customs. It would be democratic in the sense that the rulers at all levels of society would be elected by the people. The *ulamas* would participate heavily and guide the democratic process of such a political system, particularly at grass-root levels. They could become candidates to represent the prople in the new Iranian *Majlis* (a proposed unicameral Parliament). Islamic law would be the principal basis of governing the society. Prohibitions on drinking, gambling, and banking interest would be enforced on a nation-wide scale. Western-educated and Iranian-educated specialists would serve as technocrats, performing the major administrative tasks of governing the nation. Secular law may co-exist with Islamic law, where it does not conflict with Islamic law. Prominent religious leaders, particularly the well-known ayatollahs, would act as "critics" of government policy, with an explicit, established right to challenge and veto those policies which in their opinion contradict the teachings of Islam.

The foreign policy characteristics of an Islamic republic would reflect and include: (a) Nationalism and anti-colonialism, eventually with a conciliatory approach toward the United States and possibly a noncommittal view toward the Soviet Union. In general, "nonalignment" would characterize its foreign policy posture. (b) Protection of Iran's independence and territorial integrity would have priority over all other elements in the substantive and procedural aspects of Iranian foreign policy. (c) Iran's ties with the Moslem nations of the Middle East, North Africa and the rest of the Third World would expand and improve to a considerable extent. (d) Iran's relations with Israel and South Africa have been severed. No oil will be shipped from Iran to these two countries. (e) Oil may also be used as a political "weapon" against Israel's supporters. (f) Selective, measured support will be provided to various revolutionary groups in the Middle East, with considerable support for Yasir Arafat's Al Fatah branch of the PLO. As a minimum, Iran's support for the PLO would be financial, spiritual, and political. Such support might include sending Moslem revolutionaries, such as members from the *Mujahedeen Khalgh* to participate in pro-PLO operations. (g) Iran has renounced the bilateral Egyptian-Israeli peace treaty and has severed diplomatic relations with Egypt; however, Iran's position vis-a-vis the steadfast Arab front, which rejects the Egyptian-Israeli peace treaty, will probably remain ambiguous. (h) Iran's bilateral defense executive agreement of 1959 with the United States may be renounced, provided that the Islamic Republic could also renounce the 1921 Soviet-Iranian Treaty as well. Iran's multilateral defense tie with the West through the Central Treaty Organization (CENTO) has already been renounced. (i) Iran's commercial relations with the West, particularly with the United States, would decline, with France as a possible exception to this rule, because of Ayatollah Khomeini's brief exile in France and the rapport that has since been established between France and Iran. (j) Iran's arms procurement policies have changed. There will be a considerable reduction in the quantity of arms to be procured. However, spare parts for the U.S. equipment already purchased by and in the hands of the Iranian military could be purchased from the United States. (k) Iran's overall production of oil would be sustained at lower rates than in the past, and sold at considerably higher prices. The West may no longer perceive Iran as a dependable source of oil as it has in the past, and Iran's role as the self-proclaimed policeman of the Gulf would end.

(2) *Continued instability and unrest*

It is conceivable that Ayatollah Khomeini's call to all Iranians to lay down their arms and to unite may continue to go unheeded, and that the nation may fail to return to normalcy. In such a setting, it is conceivable that diverse ethnic groups in a spectrum from the right to the far left, could continue to fuel instability and unrest, a situation which could lead to coups and counter-coups in Iran, probably emanating from junior officer ranks of the Islamic republic's armed forces. Ultimately, what is important is that which takes place after such a chaotic period. Therefore, the unfortunate, short-range consequences of such an era would not, in themselves, indicate the direction of Iran's foreign and domestic policy. These policies will be determined by those who take control of the government of Iran after such a chaotic period.

(3) *People's democratic Islamic republic*

It is conceivable that the Iranian people may arrive at a government in which all elements of that nation, to include Marxists and revolutionary groups, would play a role. Traditionally, once Marxists gain control of a nation's power structure, they would not relinquish their power in the political process. Such a process in Iran could ultimately lead to the creation of a people's democratic Islamic republic, which could be somewhat similar to the People's Democratic Republic of Yemen (PDRY), but with a stronger Islamic flavor. The internal, defense and foreign policy postures of Iran under such a system would be leftist, Islamic, and conceivably pro-Soviet.

A pro-Soviet People's democratic Islamic republic would have negative implications for the pro-Western nations of the Persian Gulf/Arabian Peninsula area in particular and the Middle East in general. It would tilt the balance of power equilibrium in favor of radical, pro-Soviet nations in the area. Finally, a pro-Soviet Iran, along with a pro-Soviet Afghanistan and the People's Democratic Republic of Yemen, would pose serious threats to traditional, conservative, pro-Western regimes in the Middle East, particularly if the Soviet Union persuaded such an Iranian regime to pursue an active revolutionary role in the area.

CURRENT ASSESSMENT

The departure of the Shah from Iran on January 17, 1979, and Ayatollah Khomeini's return to Iran on January 31, 1979, are two of the highest points in the culmination of the Iranian revolution: both developments mark the 'success of the Khomeini-inspired and led revolution. Ayatollah Khomeini has left Tehran for the holy city of Qum, but he will remain the "guiding light" and the "father" of the Iranian revolution. Some of the people of Iran have bestowed the highest and most respectful Shia religious title of *imam* to him, while other, more cautious, Iranians refer to him as *nayeb al-imam*. He will likely remain the most important personality in the planning and implementation of an Islamic republic in Iran. The resumption of the flow of oil began on March 5, 1979, and is expected to continue in the future, but at a lower volume than during the Pahlavi regime.

In February-March 1979, the Prime Minister-designate Mehdi Bazargan's government served as the *de jure* government in Iran, while the *de facto* operations of governing the country were in the hands of the revolutionary committees (*Komitahaye Enghelabi*). These committees often acted autonomously, receiving direction from Ayatollah Khomeini's Revolutionary Council's Central Committee (*Komiteh Markazi*), which is, after Ayatollah Khomeini the most important revolutionary "guide" in Iran. Bazargan had no authority over dealings with the revolutionary courts, which by early April 1979 had sent about 158 people before the firing squads.[11] Bazargan emphasized the need to end the "spirit of revenge," implicitly suggesting an end to trials and executions of people who had served under the Shah.[12]

In late April 1979, Ayatollah Mahdavi Khani, the Supreme Commander of Iran's *Kometeh Markazi* (Central Committee) announced a purge of the revolutionary committees, and their phase-out to be implemented along with the reestablishment of a national police force throughout Iran. The national police force would be constituted from members of the revolutionary committees.[13] Also in late April 1979, a draft to Iran's constitution was published which effectively banned Communists from holding high office in Iran.

According to Iran's draft constitution, the president of the Islamic republic is to be a Shia Moslem, a nationalist--without "leftist" or "rightist" leanings. He cannot be a "follower of any misleading ideology."[14] Ayatollah Khomeini will have no official rule under the newly revised constitution, a preliminary draft of which was published in May 1979. Elections for a Council of Experts were held in August 1979, and that body will draft the final version of the constitution.[15] The final draft of the revised constitution of Iran will probably reflect the views of the pro-Khomeini 73-member Council of Experts. According to one Iranian constitutional scholar who has seen the preliminary drafted constitution, the new articles appear to be less "liberal" than the 1906 Constitution. The preliminary draft provides for a council of religious leaders to have the ultimate authority on deciding whether the laws are validly based on Islamic laws or not.[16]

Based on what has happened in Iran since the return of Ayatollah Khomeini, it appears that the chances of the successful establishment of a traditional Islamic republic in Iran are relatively high. However, the principal test of the capability of the Islamic republic will come in the future over the way the Islamic republic would deal with Iran's minorities. A successful effort to consolidate the Arabs, Baluchis, and Kurds into the mainstream of Iranian life will be a major hallmark of the ultimate success of the Islamic republic. Likewise, a failure to provide the minorities with the basic amenities which are provided to others in Iran could enhance separatism among them. Iran's dealings with its minorities will also dictate the degree of the potential implications of the revolution for other countries in the Middle East who have large ethnic minorities, including Israel.

In late April 1979, the Kurdistan Democratic Party (KDP), representing the Kurds in Iran, announced that fierce fighting had resumed in Iran's northwestern provinces between Kurdish tribesmen and the Iranian Army, which was assisted by Azerbaijanis and Islamic revolutionaries.[17] It is quite likely that a united front by the Iranian Army, the Azerbaijanis and the Islamic revolutionaries will eventually contain the Kurds in Iran.[18]

The three million ethnic Arabs of Iran reside predominantly in the oil-rich southwestern province of Khuzistan. They have threatened to leave Iran, unless stability is restored to Khuzistan.[19] Some of the leaders of Iran's ethnic Arabs have openly demanded autonomy, a revival of Arab culture, and the right to educate their children in Arabic in Iran's public (government) schools. Furthermore, while allowing Tehran to maintain control over foreign and economic policies, some ethnic Arab leaders prefer to control regional planning in the province of Khuzistan.[20] The Baluchis in southeastern Iran and the Turkomans in northwestern Iran have also demanded various degrees of autonomy for themselves in their regions of Iran.

While the forces favoring the establishment of an Islamic republic have achieved victory in ousting the Shah and in establishing an Islamic republic in Iran, the struggle to unite the nation and to consolidate the revolution continues. In a nation divided by ethnic groups and ideologies, the attainment of unity must remain a long term objective rather than an immediate goal. The mere expression of slogans of *itihad, mobarezeh va piroozi* (unity, struggle and victory)—slogans which have been seen on a daily basis in Iran's major urban centers—will not result in the consolidation of power in that country. These remain national aspirations. While the new regime aspires for unity, its actions in leading a diverse, heterogeneous people toward that objective also tend to indicate its ultimate success.

POTENTIAL IMPLICATIONS OF THE IRANIAN REVOLUTION

What are some of the potential, real, and perceived economic, political, and security implications of the Iranian revolution for the major countries bordering Iran in particular and the Middle East in general, considering that in the Middle East the perception of what is happening is, perhaps, just as important as what is really taking place. In general terms, the Iranian revolution should be carefully studied by students of polical change and modernization, as a relevant model of revolution particularly for the Islamic nations of the Third World. The Iranian revolution may shatter the fundamental assumptions of the Western-oriented contemporary theories of comparative politics and modernization. It has already seriously threatened the validity and applicability of the secular model of development, particularly for the Moslem nations of Africa, Asia, and the Middle East. For alarmists, awesome fears of instability, crisis, and upheaval are prevalent in the weak, vulnerable, and highly penetrable social and political systems of the conservative, traditional countries of the Islamic world. The potential midrange implications of such developments could be incalculable.

Serious questions arise regarding the prospects for U.S. and Soviet influence in the Middle East. Iran, as one of the pillars of the U.S. "twin pillars" diplomacy in this area, will no longer act as an ally of the West, and the possible lack of attaining a comprehensive peace settlement in the Arab-Israeli zone of conflict will further reduce U.S. influence in the region.

It is clear that in the period after the Iranian revolution any long range U.S. national security policy must be aimed toward maintaining a power equilibrium in the Middle East favorable to the West. U.S. ability to maintain a favorable equilibrium with the Soviet Union in the Middle East will, in turn, influence the changing balance of power between revolutionary versus conservative regimes in the area. Options for the United States in seeking a new pattern in the region could include: (1) U.S. assurances of expanded supply of arms for U.S. friends; (2) more frequent appearances of U.S. naval forces in the Indian Ocean; (3) expansion of Diego Garcia; and (4) possible establishment of naval and air base(s) in the Middle East.[21]

In terms of Western dependence on Middle Eastern oil, in late December 1978, John Lichtblau, the Executive Director of the Petroleum Research Foundation, stated that: "With the Iranian production, we had a very comfortable margin. If something were now to go wrong somewhere else, it could be a disaster."[22] According to energy specialists, thereafter, the supply-demand equation for oil was "balanced on a knife edge, at the mercy of events and the large exporters."[23]

The December 1978 oil price increase of the Organization of Petroleum Exporting Countries (OPEC) was higher than expected. The higher increase has been attributed to the oil shortage created by the substantial decline in Iran's output. As a result, Americans faced a tougher year than expected, particularly in their attempts to control inflation, reduce unemployment and reduce a potential economic stagnation. The higher cost of oil will have a pervasive impact on transportation, housing and literally all sectors of the U.S. economy. The 1979 federal budget deficit may rise beyond the $30 billion ceiling pledged by the Carter administration. The 1978 federal budget deficit was close to $40 billion.[24]

James R. Schlesinger, the Energy Secretary, stated in early February 1979 that the Iranian revolution has resulted in an oil crisis "more serious" than the selective Arab oil embargo of 1973. Schlesinger accurately predicted mandatory closure of gas stations on Sundays by summer of 1979 as a necessity, if the Iranian oil shortfall continued. During the height of the Iranian upheavals, Saudi Arabia produced 10.5 million barrels per day (mbpd) in order to reduce the impact of the total cutbacks in Iran's oil exports; however, thereafter, Saudi Arabia placed a ceiling of 9.5 mbpd on its oil production, thus further increasing the already global shortage in the supply of oil.[25]

John F. O'Leary, U.S. Deputy Energy Secretary, warned in early February 1979 that Iran's revolution will prompt some of the other major oil producers to restrict future production in the midrange period, and to adopt conservative production policies. Both O'Leary and Schlesinger stated that Iran's renewed oil production will probably not exceed 4 million barrels per day (mbpd) again. Prior to the revolution, Iran produced as much as 6.5 mbpd. O'Leary viewed Iran's revolution as the forerunner of "the disappearance of the chronic surpluses that have dominated the oil market."[26]

Iran's revolution will probably have an impact on the Moslem Turkic and Asian minorities of the Soviet Union. The degree and extent of its impact, however, remains to be determined. These minorities have the highest birthrate in the Soviet Union. As such, the long-range implications of the resurgence of Islam would be noted and carefully observed by the Kremlin. The issue of Azerbaijani, Kurdish, and Turkoman separatism could also have a serious spillover impact on the U.S.S.R., because of the presence of these people in the Soviet Union. On the other hand, the Soviet Union may have opportunities to exploit these minorities in Iran to the advantage of the Soviet Union.

Afghanistan. The uprising by the tribal elements and Islamic militants in Afghanistan will be influenced by the outcome of events in Iran. In early May 1979, reports indicated that over 3,000 Soviet advisers, technicians, and military personnel were helping Afghanistan to fight against the uprising.[27]

A prolonged tribal Islamic rebellion in Afghanistan will pose a serious threat to the legitimacy of the leftist regime in Afghanistan. It may lead to an even greater involvement of Soviet advisers, technicians and equipment in Afghanistan, testing the Soviet will to assist a friendly regime which has become increasingly unpopular in its own nation. Furthermore, the Pashtu people in northwestern Pakistan will probably continue to fight both the Pakistani as well as Afghan forces for an autonomous Pakhtunistan.

What would be the impact of the Iranian revolution and the Afghan rebellion on India and Pakistan? To what extent would the Islamic Republic align itself with the Moslem countries in the area? What would be the impact of a close alignment between Iran and other revolutionary regimes of the area on Saudi Arabia and the small vulnerable sheikhdoms of the Gulf area? How would such an alignment impact on U.S. influence in this critical region of the world? The answer to these questions can only be given in time, as the Islamic Republic of Iran proceeds to solidify its ties abroad. However, it is clear that the future Iran is bound to be more revolutionary and Islamic. As such Iran will inevitably draw itself closer to the Islamic nations in the area, particularly to those adjacent to Iran, such as Pakistan, and probably at the expense of Iran's ties with non-Moslem nations farther away such as India. The Shah's unrealistic visions of an Indian Ocean littoral's common market, his grand plans for an ambitious role for the Iranian Navy in cooperation with India's Navy in the Indian Ocean, and the Shah's advocacy for Iran and India to patrol jointly the Indian Ocean are of course shattered.[28]

Egypt. As one of the leading nations in the Middle East and Africa, Egypt plays a key role in the Third World. The resurgence of Islam may have its greatest potential implication in Egypt, which is a leading nation in Sunni Islam, while the implications of the Iranian revolution on the Egyptian political system could be minimal. So far, President Anwar Sadat's quality of personal piety, leadership, humility, and his understanding of the centrality of Islam as a way of life for Egyptians has prevented the development of any serious politico-religious threat to the legitimacy of his rule. However, rising expectation, mounting economic pressures, under-employment, shortage of housing, and other socio-economic ills facing Egypt will seriously test the legitimacy of Sadat's government in Egypt.

Egypt and Saudi Arabia once regarded Iran as an anchor of stability and pro-Western influence in the entire Middle East. The Shah's collapse and drastic changes in Iran's foreign and defense policies are of prime concern to the Wahhabi dynasty, President Sadat, and other pro-Western regimes in the Middle East.

Iraq and Turkey. In mid-April 1979, Iraq and Turkey reached an agreement to act jointly on the Kurdish issue. Bulent Ecevit, Turkish Premier, stated that containing Kurdish separatism was one of his government's primary tasks. The agreement between Iraq and Turkey over the Kurds was probably a response to major concessions made by Iran's Islamic republic to the Kurds, in order to consolidate Iran's revolution and maintain national unity. As a result of the events in Iran, Kurdish nationalism and separatism was sparked in both Iraq and Turkey.

Approximately ten million Kurds now live in an area which covers parts of northwestern Iran, northeastern Iraq, and southeastern Turkey.[29] Iraq and Turkey have dealt with the Kurds differently. Iraq, for example, used 30 percent of its developmental funds in 1978 for the Kurdish areas. According to Baha Ahmad, a Kurd and the Governor of Arbil, Iraq, the Kurds". . . have been raised up, like all the people in Iraq and even more."[30] The Iraqi regime of Ahmad Hassan Bakr poured economic relief and development funds into the Kurdish areas of northeastern Iraq, allowed the Kurds to have a semblance of autonomy, and recruited Kurds into the Baath Party (the ruling party in Iraq) in order to reduce Kurdish separatist tendencies. The town of Arbil, located east of Mosul, is the nominal capital of the Iraqi Kurds. Mosul lies in the mountains of northeastern Iraq. Iraq has built villages such as Khobata, located between Arbil and Mosul, for the Kurds. Some Western observers suspected that these villages were like the reservation was for the American Indians.[31]

Is the Soviet Union fomenting Kurdish nationalism and separatism, in order to establish a pro-Soviet Kurdish state in the region? Celal Talabani, one of the principal Kurdish rebel leaders in Sulaimaniyah, Iraq, is a self-proclaimed Marxist, who commands a contingent of 1500 fighters, armed with Soviet-made automatic weapons and artillery. According to Talabani, "the downfall of the Shah has liberated [Kurdish] forces from one front."[32] So far, however, there is no evidence of Soviet direct activities in support of the Kurds in Iraq; however, assertions regarding covert Soviet activities in the Middle East are abundant. For example, Senator Kamran Inan of Turkey, who is a Kurd, maintains that the Soviet Union is definitely encouraging and assisting Kurdish separatists in this area.[33]

Aside from the Kurds, Iraq also has a considerable Shia population. According to one estimate about 50 percent of Iraq's population are Shia Moslems. They are particularly strong in the Shia holy cities of Karbala and Najaf, which were sites of pro-Khomeini religious demonstrations in the spring of 1979. The top Iraqi leadership is largely Sunni from Takrit, a small town about 100 miles north of Baghdad.[34] A tightly-knit familial group of Takritis controls Iraq through the Baath Socialist Party. The impact of the Iranian revolution on the Shias of Iraq and on the legitimacy of Iraq's leadership could be significant in the mid-range period.

The Kurds and the Shias (Alawis) are viewed as the potential transmitters of the implications of the Iranian revolution in Turkey. An estimated five million Kurds reside in Turkey, and about 20 percent of Turkey's population are Shia Moslems.[35] Despide Ankara's promises of economic relief and assistance to the Kurds, it appears unlikely that meaningful assistance would be forthcoming because of Turkey's overall economic difficulties.

The Shia (Alawis) of Turkey reside principally in the eastern provinces of Turkey and in its major cities. The Shias of Turkey are liberal, progressive element of society. They are reformists. The pervasive religious aspects of the Iranian revolution may have some impact on Turkey's Shia population, despite the fact that the Turkish political process has moved considerably away from religion, as exemplified by the reduced representation in the Parliament by the Turkish Unity Party which is a Shia party. Overall, the religious vote in Turkey is less than 10 percent. As such, it is not a significant factor in Turkey's political process. Furthermore, both Turkey and Iraq lack national focus in a charismatic personality such as Ayatollah Khomeini, to threaten the existing government and reawaken the masses. Finally, Turkey is a functioning democratic society capable of handling such threats in an institutionalized manner. Despite such an assurance, however, Turkey faces serious political problems arising from the growing polarization between the extreme ideological left and the religious right. In addition, expanded terrorism, unemployment, rampant inflation, shortage of housing, decline in public services, and an almost bankrupt national economy could seriously threaten Ecevit's government in the near future. For example, the rate of inflation in Turkey in 1978-79 exceeded 50 percent *per annum,* and the Turkish government lacks sufficient foreign exchange reserves to pay for its severely needed imports.[36]

In military-strategic terms, the Iranian revolution and the withdrawal of Iran and Pakistan from the Central Treaty Organization (CENTO) have led to the withdrawal of Turkey from CENTO and its *de facto* dissolution.[37] The loss of U.S. electronic surveillance sites in Iran has made U.S. electronic listening posts in Turkey more significant, particularly for the purpose of assisting the United States in verifying a new strategic arms limitation treaty (SALT). In addition, it is highly likely that U.S.-Turkish negotiations over the status of U.S. installations and military presence in Turkey would be modified and supplemented, in order to emphasize a "full-fledged" partnership between the Turks and the West.[38] For Iraq, the spill-over potentials of the Iranian revolution into Iraq and its impact on Iraq's Shia Moslem fundamentalists and Kurdish separatists may require the use of Syria as a strategic depth. Both Iraq and Syria view each other as strategic depths for threats emanating from two potential zones of conflict, the Arab Israeli zone to their west and the Iranian theater to their east. In the renouncement of Iran's commitment to play a policeman role in the Persian Gulf area, Iraq may seek to fill some of the void created by the Islamic republic's plans to scale down Iran's military presence in the Gulf area. The impact of a potentially active and expanded Iraqi military presence in the Gulf area would depend upon Iraq's policy objectives, methods of implementing such plans, and Iraq's relations with its neighbors, and the Peninsula Arab's perception of Iraq's role. With a substantially reduced Iranian presence the indigenous balance of power equilibrium in the Gulf area will undoubtedly change. If the Islamic republic of Iran aligns itself with Iraq and Syria, ideologically and militarily, that would drastically alter the pro-Western balance of power in the Middle East and could have immediate consequences for fragile, pro-Western, conservative regimes of the area as well as for the Arab-Israeli zone of conflict. In this context, the implantation of the PLO mission in Ahwaz, Iran, close to the oilfields of Iran and the Arab world was a psychological boost for the radical Arabs, with an explicit impact in the minds of the Arabs regarding a potential major shift in favor of revolutionary forces in the Middle East.[39]

According to Henry Kissinger, the oil-rich states of the Persian Gulf area may doubt U.S resolve and support and seek reassurances in Moscow or Iraq, as a result of the Shah's departure.[40] If Iraq and Syria move really closer to each other, the conservative governments of the Arabian Peninsula may feel its impact in their countries. Israel would also be influenced by such a strategic development in its Eastern front.

Israel and the PLO. The linkages between most of the nations of the Gulf area and the Arab nations opposing the bilateral peace treaty between Egypt and Israel will solidify and expand as long as a comprehensive peace settlement does not appear to be forthcoming. The Islamic republic of Iran has also interjected itself into the politics of the Arab-Israeli zone by breaking off its diplomatic relations with Egypt; renouncing Iran's ties with Israel; announcing its support for the PLO; and by halting the shipment of Iranian oil to Israel.

Iran's new relationship with Israel has shifted from a discreet entente to open animosity. Pars News Agency, the official press agency of Iran, on February 18, 1979, stated that termination of all relations with Israel and the full support of the PLO were cornerstones of Iran's foreign policy.[41]

Prior to the revolution, over 26 million barrels of Iranian oil per year were shipped to Israel. Since then Israel has purchased 10 percent of its oil needs from Mexico and the rest from spot purchases at substantially higher than OPEC's-posted prices, a situation which has left its impact on Israel's economy.

As a result of the severance of relations with Iran, Israel has lost the principal source for import of 60 percent of its oil needs and a lucrative contract market for services. Iran used to import over $100 million of goods from Israel and EL AL had five scheduled weekly flights from Tel Aviv to Tehran. Iran and Turkey were the only countries in the Middle East which dealt with Israel. Israel, as a result of its bilateral peace treaty with Egypt, has probably written Egypt off its list of adversaries, but may have to add Iran to that list.

Yasir Arafat, the leader of the Palestine Liberation Organization, was the first foreign leader to visit Ayatollah Khomeini in Iran. Arafat during his February 1979 visit stated that the Iranian Revolution has "turned upside down" the balance of power in the Middle East. He received a pledge from the Ayatollah that Iran would "turn to the issue of victory over Israel" after the Islamic Republic consolidated its power.[42]

Saudi Arabia The geopolitical realities of Saudi Arabia's location place this Kingdom in a precarious position. The Kingdom is located between three zones of instability and change: First, the Iranian situation in the northern half of the Gulf, with its uncertain aftermath; second, the continuing dispute in the southern parts of the Arabian Peninsula between North and South Yemen, and the potentials for another uprising in Oman against Sultan Qabus; third, the Arab-Israeli conflict, and potentials for its extension into the Arabian Peninsula; finally, crises as a result of inter-Arab or intra-Arab disputes between, e.g., Iraq and Kuwait. The Saudi leadership is quite concerned about adventurism and instability in the periphery of the Kingdom because of its potential spillover impacts into Saudi Arabia.

Internally, the Saudi leadership has the wide support of its people. It is a respected, legitimate regime. The religious institutions in the Kingdom are a part of the establishment. They even participate in deciding who the next King would be. As such, Saudi Arabia has a high likelihood of internal political stability during the midrange period. The only conceivable internal challenges to the Saud family may arise from within the royal family or from the growing Saudi military. Some analysts contend that the growing foreign workers which include over one million Yemenis may also serve as a fifth column in the Kingdom.

Palace politics in Saudi Arabia remain unknown to outsiders. American intelligence specialists have likened the discovery of what goes on in Riyadh to "the secrecy in Moscow and Peking."[43] Palace politics is discussed in great secrecy and confidentiality among the key personalities involved. In April 1979 Western reporters wrote of palace strife in the Saudi royal family between Prince Abdullah and his brother Prince Fahd, who is second in power after King Khalid. Prince Abdullah vehemently denied the rumor, and American officials agreed with Prince Abdullah's views on this matter.[44]

The withdrawal of Iranian forces from Oman, as a result of the Iranian upheavals, could lead toward a re-activation of the revolt in Oman. The People's Democratic Republic of Yemen (PDRY), otherwise known as South Yemen, and Cubans with Russian weapons, could expand their activities in support of radical groups in the Gulf and the Arabian Peninsula. Such developments will be viewed as threatening Saudi Arabia, thus pressuring the Saudis to play the role of a policeman in the Gulf and the Peninsula, particularly in the absence of such a role played by Iran. That could trigger a multiple increase in the level of Saudi arms acquisitions from the United States.

In summary, the Iranian revolution of 1978-79, along with the bilateral peace treaty between Egypt and Israel, mark the dawn of a new era in the Middle East--an era in which legitimacy, public consensus, and popular support, rather than military might and external ties, will be the principal criteria for the capability of Middle Eastern leaders to maintain their power.

NOTES

1. Ahmad Eqbal, "Iran: A Possible Landmark," *The New York Times,* April 15, 1979, p. 23.
2. *Ibid.*
3. Leonard Binder, "Revolution in Iran: Red, White, Blue or Black," *The Bulletin of the Atomic Scientists,* January 1979, pp. 52 and 54.
4. Hamid Algar, "The Oppositional Role of the Ulama in Twentieth-Century Iran," in Nikki R. Keddie, ed., *Scholars, Saints and Sufis: Muslim Religious Institutions in the Middle East Since 1500,* Berkeley: University of California Press, 1972, pp. 231-32
5. *Ibid.,* pp. 231-255.
6. According to the Holy Koran (Verse 28:4) the return of Imam Mahdi, the Twelfth Imam, will result in the redemption and elevation of those who have been oppressed—an aspiration which reflects an inherent desire among Shia Moslems for social justice.
7. Richard Cottam, *Nationalism in Iran,* Pittsburgh, PA: University of Pittsburgh Press, p. 284.
8. *Ibid.*
9. Shahriar Rouhani, "Executions in Iran," *The Washington Post,* April 27, 1979.
10. John Kifner, "Ayatollah's Killers Send Chill Through Iran Leaders," *The New York Times,* May 3, 1979, p. 3.
11. William Branigan, "Reports of Attack on Prime Minister Set Tehran on Edge," *The Washington Post,* April 25, 1979, p. 18.
12. *Ibid.*
13. Youssef M. Ibrahim, "Iranians Decide to Purge and Phase Out Vigilantes," *The New York Times,* April 26, 1979, p. 1.
14. William Branigan, "Draft Charter for iran Would Bar Communists," *The Washington Post,* April 30, 1979, p. 22.
15. *Ibid.* See also youssef M. Ibrahim, "Election in Iran: Khomeini's Victory May Prove Costly, *The New York Times* (August 8, 1979,), p. 4.
16. William Branigan, "Draft Charter for Iran Would Bar Communists," *The Washington Post,* April 30, 1979, p. 22.
17. William Branigan, "Iranian Kurds Say Army Has Joined Drive Against Them," *The Washington Post,* April 26, 1979, p. 29.
18. Youssef M Ibrahim, "Iran Reports Cease-Fire in Area Where Kurds and Turks Clashed," *The New York Times,* April 27, 1979, p. 13.
19. *Ibid.*
20. *Ibid.*
21. Bernard Weintraub, "Increased US Role in the Mideast is Urged," *The New York Times,* February 19, 1979, p. 3.
22. Steven Rattner, "200 American Workers. US Weighs Sending Ships to Area; Indefinite Shutdown Feared," *The New York Times,* December 29, 1978, pp. 1 and 6.
23. *Ibid.*
24. Harry B. Ellis, "Oil Costs Cut Into US Growth," *The Christian Science Monitor,* December 21, 1978, pp. 1 and 9.
25. "Schlesinger Pessimistic on Iran Oil," *The Washington Post,* February 8, 1979, p. 8.
26. J.P. Smith, "Iran Upheaval Seen Leading Others to Lower Oil Exports," *The Washington Post,* February 15, 1979, p. 16.
27. "Afghanistan Said to Obtain Soviet Copter Gunships," *The New York Times,* May 4, 1979, p. 5.
28. Mohan Ram, "India Anxious Over Impact of Turmoil in Iran: Fall of Shah Could Shift South Asian Strategies, *The Christian Science Monitor,* December 28. 1978, p. 4.
29. John Lawton, "Turkey, Iraq to Act Jointly on Kurds," *The Washington Post,* April 18, 1979, p. 14.

30. Thomas W. Lippman, "Kurds Resettled by Iraq Show Little of Fiery Independence," *The Washington Post*, April 18, 1979, p. 15.
31. *Ibid.*
32. John Lawton, "Turkey, Iraq to Act Jointly on Kurds," *The Washington Post*, April 18, 1979, p. 14.
33. *Ibid.*
34. Bosth Ahamd Hassan al Bakr, President of Iraq, and Sadam Hossein, Vice President, are from Takrit, The Minister of Defense, Adana Khary Allah, is the son-in-law of Hassan al Bakr and brother-in-law of Saddam Hossein. See, Joseph Kraft, "Iraq: Fending Off Ferment," *The Washington Post*, April 24, 1979, p. 19.
35. John Lawton, "Turkey, Iraq to Act Jointly on Kurds," *The Washington Post*, April 18, 1979, p. 14.
36. See Michael Getler, "Political Violence, Economic Ills Stir Fears for Turkey's Future," *The Washington Post*, February 5, 1979. p. 1.
37. In early February, 1979, Ahmad Mir Fendereski, Iran's Foreign Minister under the Bakhtiar's premiership, stated that his government has decided to withdraw Iran from the Central Treaty Organization because, as he put it, "the continuing presence of Iran in CENTO is inexplicable in the context of Iran's new foreign policy." See Jonathan C. Randall, "Problems Seen No Matter Who Governs in Iran," *The Washington Post*, February 7, 1979, p. 14.
38. Michael Getter, "Americans Tread Warily in Turkish Base Talks," *The Washington Post*, February 9, 1979, p. 15.
39. Interview with John Cooley of *The Christain Science Monitor* in early May, 1979, at the US Army War College, Carlisle Barracks, PA.
40. "Kissinger Says Weak CIA Led to Shah's Departure," *The Washington Post*, February 9, 1979, p. 19.
41. "More Top Officials Arrested in Iran," *The New York Times*, February 19, 1979, p. 6.
42. James M. Markham, "Arafat, in Iran, Reports Khomeini Pledges Aid for Victory Over Israel," *The New York Times*, February 19, 1979, p. 1.
43. Bernard Gwertzman, "Saudi Rift on Egypt Is Denied by Prince," *The New York Times*, April 30, 1979, p. 2.
44. *Ibid.*

III. IRAN AS A POLITICAL VARIABLE: PATTERNS AND PROSPECTS

Charles G. MacDonald

Revolutionary Iran, with its ideology of revolution that attacks Western-style modernization in general and American and Israeli "imperialism" in particular, has come to undermine stability in the Persian Gulf and to threaten Arab governments in the Gulf and throughout the Middle East. The uncertainties emerging from the Iranian revolution, accentuated by Iran's internal power struggle, and broadened by the Iran-Iraq War, have placed Iran at the focal point of world attention. The question of Iran's future policy has become crucial to the West because of Iran's strategic location on the world's oil jugular, the Strait of Hormuz, and the continued dependence of the West on Persian Gulf oil. While many in the West are trying to understand and predict Iranian policy through the study of traditional Islamic precepts and through the too often wishful thinking sensationalized by the press, the probable direction of Iran's policy could be more easily approached through an examination of the dynamic political relationships that exist in the Persian Gulf, together with the nature of Iran's militant, but uncomplicated, ideology of revolution.

The equivocal statements from various Iranian government officials since the success of the Islamic revolution have served to keep potential enemies off balance, including those in the West, in the Persian Gulf, and within Iran. Fluctuating policy statements from Iran reflect the multiple power centers that have been carefully used and balanced against each other by Ayatollah Khomeini.[1] Representing the only authoritative voice in Iran, Ayatollah Khomeini has kept the internal power centers in balance not simply to maintain control of the revolution, but also to create time for molding the type of revolution that he desires.

Presently, Iran is at an important crossroads in its revolution. Iran's first Constitutional Government has been selected (with only a few positions still contested). Perhaps the most important decision to be made is whether Iran should work actively to export its revolution to other Gulf states and possibly beyond, or should it consolidate its successes within Iran. The question that faces Iran is not unlike that faced by the Soviet Union after the initial success of the Bolshevik Revolution.[2] Should Iran attempt to spread its revolution or should it attempt to solidify the accomplishments of the revolution within Iran? Can the revolution survive in one country or must the energies of the revolution be fueled by expansion?

The answer lies in the nature of the political relationships that exist in the Persian Gulf on one hand, and in the relationship between Iran's internal political developments and its foreign policy goals on the other. Iran's role in the Persian Gulf is that of a political variable, influenced by both the political forces at work within the Persian Gulf context and the philosophy of revolution emerging from Iran's internal power struggle.

POLITICAL DYNAMICS IN THE PERSIAN GULF

Iran's policy toward its Arab neighbors is tied to a complex of underlying political conflicts found in the Persian Gulf context.[3] These underlying political conflicts are dynamic in character and often overlap. The result is constantly changing political relationships. Political interests often simultaneously coincide and conflict. States's relationships with other states can shift dramatically depending upon the priorities of the day. Generally speaking, political interaction in the Persian Gulf is based upon four fundamental political conflicts: (1) the struggle between nationalism and imperialism; (2) the struggle between rival nationalisms; (3) the conflict between traditionalism and revolution; and (4) the substantive conflict between states over territory and resources. These four underlying political conflicts are further complicated by the United States-Soviet rivalry, the Arab-Israeli conflict, and the rivalry between oil-exporting and oil-importing states. The relationships between Iran and its Persian Gulf neighbors, as well as between Iran and outside powers, are dependent upon the dynamic political contest of the Gulf.

Iranian Nationalism Versus Imperialism

The Iranian nation has a long history of foreign domination and exploitation. The conflict between Iranian nationalism and imperialism has been present throughout the twentieth century, making Iranians especially sensitive to threats to their sovereignty and territorial integrity. In 1907 the Anglo-Russian Agreement essentially partitioned Iran (Persia) into British and Russian spheres of influence.[4] During World War I, despite Iran's declaring its neutrality, parts of Iran saw battles between foreign armies. After the war the Treaty of Friendship between Persia and the Russian Socialist Federal Soviet Republic was signed at Moscow in February 1921.[5] Article 6 of the treaty provided Russia with "the right to advance her troops into the Persian interior for the purpose of carrying out the military operations necessary for its defense." In August 1941 British and Soviet forces invaded and occupied Iran.[6] The failure of the Soviet Union to withdraw its forces promptly created one of the first problems with which the fledgling United Nations had to deal. Soviet troops were removed only after President Truman issued an ultimatum to Stalin.[7] The Anglo-Iranian oil crisis beginning in 1951 represented a major thrust of Iranian nationalism against what it saw as British exploitation.

Traditionally, the Iranians have looked to the United States as a balance against the Soviets and the British. The fall of the Shah in 1979 and the association of the United States with him, especially after the C.I.A.-sponsored coup of 1953, brought charges of imperialism aimed at the United States. In fact, Ayatollah Khomeini's exile was the result of, *inter alia*, his criticism of exterritorial privileges granted to American military personnel that, in effect, gave them diplomatic immunity.[8] In 1964 Khomeini charged that "this most disgraceful decree" had placed "the Iranian people under American bondage."[9] Later, his criticisms of American imperialism set the stage for the seizure of the American Embassy on 4 November 1979. In the week prior to the seizure of the hostages, Ayatollah Khomeini lashed out at the United States by claiming, "All our (Iranian) problems come from America. All the problems of the Muslims stem from America."[10] In September 1980 the *Majlis* Foreign Affairs Committee carefully drew up a list of twenty-four criminal acts that the American government "has done and is doing."[11] The struggle between Iranian nationalism and British, Soviet, and American influence has become a major component in Iran's foreign policy outlook, especially after the assumption of power by Ayatollah Khomeini.

Iranian Nationalism Versus Arab Nationalism

The struggle between nationalisms in the Persian Gulf primarily assumes the form of a rivalry between Iranian nationalism and Arab nationalism. This historical conflict predates Islam and is partly religious and partly racial in character. Although it is often tied to boundary and island disputes, it is characterized by an ancient suspicion and resentment that has surfaced periodically in the post-World War II period. While Iran has maintained a continuing dispute with Iraq, especially since 1958, Arab hostility toward Iran became manifest in the bitter controversy over the nomenclature of the Persian Gulf.[12] In a major verbal attack against Iran and the Shah, following an "alleged recognition" of Israel in 1960, President Nasser charged that Iranian leaders were "colleagues of colonialists" and maintained that the Shah had displayed hostility both toward Egypt and Arab nationalism since 1952.[13] The hostility engendered by such charges was seized upon by the Arab nationalists in their reference to the "Arab Gulf" (instead of the "Persian Gulf") and also in their claims that the Iranian province of Khuzistan, "Arabistan," was illegally occupied by Iranian "colonialists."[14] The disputes over the Shatt al-Arab River and over Bahrain, as well as many other island and boundary disputes, further complicated relations between Iran and its Arab neighbors.[15] Iran's seizure of Abu Musa and the Greater and Lesser Tumb Islands on the eve of the British departure in 1971 further fueled Arab animosity toward the Iranians. It is not insignificant that the Iran-Iraq War that began on 22 September 1980 is primarily being waged in the Iranian province of Khuzistan. Moreover, Iraq has reclaimed the entire Shatt al-Arab waterway and has called for Iran to return Abu Musa and the two Tumb Islands to Arab control.

Traditionalism Versus Revolution

The conflict between traditionalism and revolution in the Persian Gulf was initially characterized by the conflict between conservative monarchies and the forces of the left. The Iraqi coup of 1958 brought the first threat of a revolutionary ideology to the Gulf. Baathists, Nasserists, and communists all came to be regarded as threats by the conservative governments in the Gulf. Saudi Arabia fought a proxy war against Nasser's Egypt in Yemen. The Shah of Iran sent forces at the request of the Sultan of Oman to control the Dhofari rebels, who received assistance from Marxist South Yemen. The inter-Arab conflict among radical, moderate, and conservative

Arab states has been present in various forms throughout the postwar period.

The conflict between traditionalism and revolution, however, took on a new dimension in the Iranian revolution. Militant Islam came to be a potential threat to the traditional regimes on the Arab side of the Gulf and especially to the Baathist regime of Saddam Hussein in Iraq.

Territory and Resource Disputes

The fourth underlying political conflict is more substantive in nature and involves specific issue-oriented disputes between neighboring states. The disputes are often territorial in nature; many deal with competing claims to island and offshore resources. Following the British announcement in 1968 of its pending withdrawal from "East of Suez," Iran reached a number of agreements on offshore boundaries, but several problematic disputes remain.[16] Perhaps the most important offshore boundary agreement was with Saudi Arabia in 1968. Iran subsequently reached other offshore agreements with Qatar, Bahrain, Oman, and Dubai. In May 1970 Iran also relinquished its claim to Bahrain. Still remaining in dispute, however, are Abu Musa Island (Iran-Sharjah); offshore oil rights off Abu Musa (Iran-Sharjah-Umm al-Qaiwain); the Greater and Lesser Tumb Islands (Iran-Ras al-Khaimah); Iran-Abu Dhabi offshore boundary; Iran-Kuwait offshore boundary; Iran-Kuwait-Saudi Arabia Neutral Zone offshore boundary; and the Iran-Iraq boundaries. Iran did sign a comprehensive treaty with Iraq in 1975 that delimited the Shatt al-Arab River frontier and some 670 disputed land areas. Following the Iranian revolution, Iraq indicated a desire to abrogate parts of the treaty in October 1979. Iraq declared the treaty "null and void" in September 1980, following alleged Iranian violations of the 1975 agreement.

External Influences

Iranian foreign policy depends not only on the underlying political conflicts within the Gulf, but also on such external influences as the United States-Soviet rivalry, the Arab-Israeli conflict, and the conflict of interests that exists among oil importers and exporters. Each of these relationships are interrelated with the four fundamental conflicts present in the Gulf and contributes to a complex mosaic of interests in the region.

The United States-Soviet rivalry has pervaded the Gulf since World War II. It has become foremost in the minds of strategic theorists since the Soviet forces moved into Afghanistan in December 1979, and President Carter proclaimed the Carter Doctrine in his State of the Union address in January 1980. Iran has been especially sensitive to actions by both superpowers and has adamantly opposed the Soviet actions in Afghanistan. The Islamic Republic's relations with the Soviet Union have ranged from cool to hostile. On the other hand, the United States has been seen as a direct threat to the revolution since the seizure of the American hostages. Although Iran had been closely associated with the United States in a type of regional partnership and had been a member of the Baghdad Pact and CENTO the new Islamic Republic has not hesitated to denounce its past relationship with the United States. It is ironic, however, that Iran continues its traditional policy of equilibrium (*movazeneh*) and relies upon the United States for its defense against the Soviet

Union.[17] At the same time Iran looks to the Soviet Union to counter any potential American attack.[18] While the Islamic Republic seeks to maintain its distance from both superpowers, it appears that the American sanctions have greatly increased Iran's trade with the Soviet Bloc.

The Arab-Israeli conflict has added another dimension to inter-Gulf politics. Iran under the Shah had been an important supplier of oil to Israel and had renewed its friendship with Sadat's Egypt, while calling for Israel to withdraw from occupied Arab territory. The Shah had been strongly opposed to Israel's West Bank settlements. He had also stated that the next round of the Arab-Israeli conflict would find Iran on the side of the Arabs. The new Islamic Republic has called for the overthrow of President Sadat and has sided against what it views as American and Zionist "imperialism." Although revolutionary Iran has been quite ready to support the Palestine Liberation Organization in its struggle against Israel, it has not proved receptive to a Palestinian presence in Khuzistan.

The competition between oil exporting and oil importing states has juxtaposed the oil-rich Persian Gulf states against the oil-hungry West on questions of supply and price. At the same time other rivalries in the Gulf have found their way into the OPEC arena. Since Iran continues to push for higher prices as it did under the Shah's regime, it has often come to conflict with the United States and Saudi Arabia. The differences in the abilities of states to increase production relative to other states has had a major impact on intra-Gulf relations.

From this brief discussion of the political dynamics in the Persian Gulf, it should be apparent that Iranian policy has considerable room for variation. There are interests within the matrix of underlying political conflicts and external influences that suggest conflicting policies. Simultaneously, interests of Gulf states might coincide in one area and conflict in another. Before the parameters of Iranian foreign policy can be suggested, the implications of Iran's internal political developments must also be considered.

IMPLICATIONS OF INTERNAL POLITICAL DEVELOPMENTS

Apart from the political dynamics of Iran's relationships with other Gulf states is the competition for power and authority within Iran.[19] Opposition to the Shah brought together many disparate groups that had sharply contrasting views of the ideal post-Shah Iran. There were roughly four basic groups, each with numerous factions of its own contending for power. The exterme right consisted of the hardline clerics and those directly associated with Ayatollah Khomeini. The center was commonly seen as Mossadegh-style nationalists, of which there were several parties. The left was made up of the Tudeh Party, the Fedayeen, and the Mojahedin, and factions thereof. The Mojahedin proved to be difficult to define on a right to left political spectrum. They were part of both the religious right and the political left. All of the groups tended to support Ayatollah Khomeini. The fourth group instrumental in the fall of the Shah was composed of the various ethnic minorities, who did not vie for power, but rather sought increased autonomy.

Rise of the Clerics

The political situation in Iran after the success of the anti-Shah revolution saw various power centers emerge. The internal situation there was often called chaotic and anarchic by the press. While such labels appeared suitable, they did not suggest the type of equilibrium that had developed between the various power centers. In fact, the Iranian tradition of balancing competing forces was being employed masterfully by Ayatollah Khomeini. Khomeini would from time to time shift his support from one group to another, while attacking those he saw as potential threats to the revolution. Similarly, the tribal minorities and their various factions were played off against each other.

The vicissitudes of Iranian revolutionary politics appear to have resulted in the emergence of two groups--the religious-based nationalists and the fundamentalist clerics. The first group was represented by President Bani-Sadr, who received support from some groups on the left, what remained of the center, and some of the less-extreme clerics. The second group is headed by Ayatollah Beheshti and his hardline Islamic Republican Party. Its support is drawn primarily from extremist clerics. Ayatollah Khomeini has continued to alternate his support between the two groups, apparently with the desire of preventing either group from gaining too much power. It appears, however, that Iran's first Constitutional Government is controlled by hardline clerics.

Although there still remains some semblance of resistance to the religious fundamentalists by President Bani-Sadr (who refused to accept certain ministers named by Prime Minister Rajai), the power and legitimacy of the clerics have been written into the Constitution. The Assembly of Experts that revised the Constitution in the fall of 1979 undercut the power of the President and granted virtually unlimited powers to the *faqih* (leader).[20] Not only are the powers of the President essentially those of an administrator, but if something should happen to the President, the Temporary Council of the Presidency would have more power than the President normally would have. If anything were to happen to President Bani-Sadr, he would be replaced initially by a Temporary Council made up of Ayatollah Beheshti, Hojatoleslam Rafsanjani, and Prime Minister Rajai. If something should happen to Ayatollah Khomeini, a new *faqih* would be selected by an Assembly of Experts, elected according to the provisions set forth by the Council of Guardians. The head of the first Assembly of Experts, that had been responsible for revising the Constitution and granting power to the clerics and unlimited power to the *faqih,* was Ayatollah Montazeri. He has been identified as the probable successor to Ayatollah Khomeini.

Calls for the Export of Revolution

In the fall of 1979 the actions and statements of a number of fundamentalist clerics created quite a furor for the Provisional Government. In September 1979 at Talaghani's funeral Ayatollah Montazeri openly called for the export of revolution.[21] He did so with an automatic rifle in his hand. Montazeri aimed his attacks at the leaders of other Islamic states, charging, "You leaders of Islamic states cannot protect yourselves by oppressing your Moslem citizens. You cannot continue to govern through the power of the bayonet."[22] He went on to say, "Iran's Islamic revolution will be exported to all other Moslem countries,"[23] suggesting that other governments in Islamic states were keeping the proceeds from natural resources for certain "privileged groups."[24] Ebrahim Yazdi, then foreign minister, attempted to mitigate the sharpness of Montazeri's call for the export of revolution. Yazdi stated, "We do not want to export our revolution, nor do we want to send armed men to fight foreign armies. But we cannot prevent the influence of the Islamic revolution on other countries."[25]

Iran's Provisional Government later attempted to play down the statements of the hardline clerics by denying that Iran intended to export revolution and explaining away such statements as those of private citizens. In October 1979 in an interview with *An Nahar* Prime Minister Bazargan stated, "Iran has no ambitions in the Persian Gulf region and no extraterritorial interests nor does it have any plans to strike anywhere."[26]

The clerics, however, did not hesitate to continue their call for the expansion of the Islamic revolution. Also in October 1979 Ayatollah Montazeri, then Tehran's Imam Jomeh (chief cleric), claimed during Friday Prayers that calling upon other Islamic states to enforce religious law should not be considered "meddling".[27] Allameh Yaha Nouri charged that it was an Islamic duty to support revolution in the oppressed nations of the world. He stated, "What we really want is friends, not masters, and we shall encourage and support all Islamic movements in the world."[28] Ayatollah Beheshti reportedly suggested that Iran could have good relations only with those countries that were "truly Islamic," thus subtly alluding to and offending Saudi Arabia.[29]

These calls for the export of revolution followed incidents in the Gulf Sheikhdoms where representatives of Ayatollah Khomeini were expelled. Hojatoleslam Abbas Mohri was deported for making political speeches against the Kuwaiti government in the mosques in September 1979. Similarly, other Shiite representatives were expelled for political activities in Bahrain and in the United Arab Emirates.

There were also incidents in Saudi Arabia. Just prior to the seizure of the Grand Mosque in Mecca, Saudi Arabian police broke up a gathering of Iranians who had come to hear Hojatoleslam Ghaffari speak.[30] Although the seizure of the Grand Mosque on 20 November 1979 was not directly tied to any Iranian political activities, it was later reported that the takeover was tied to political discontent and had revolutionary overtones.[31] Later in November 1979 riots did break out in Shiite areas near Ras Tanura oil refinery at Qatif. The rioters called for Saudi Arabia to support the "Islamic revolution".

Iran's call for the export of revolution has been paralleled by the support for revolutionary groups and oppressed peoples around the world. The ties between Iranian revolutionaries and various national liberation movements have continued in word and deed. The first such instance was the welcoming of Yasir Arafat, Khomeini's first official state visitor. Iran joined the Non-Aligned Movement in September 1979. In October 1979 Iran's Foreign Minister Ebrahim Yazdi delivered revolutionary Iran's first major policy before the United Nations. He attacked the institution for tolerating the human rights violations of the Shah and of "other shahs".[32] He charged, "There are other peoples in the world who are being killed, imprisoned and tortured by other shahs."[33] He reiterated Iranian support for the Palestinians and the Palestine Liberation Organization in their battle against the repression of the Zionists. He called Zionism "one of the most vicious forms of racism in recorded history," maintaining that it "displaces and terrorizes human beings simply because they do not belong to a particular race and religion."[34]

In January 1980 a conference of national liberation groups was held at the seized American Embassy in Tehran. The conference chose Ayatollah Khoini as its chairman. (He is reportedly the leader of the militants that seized the embassy and has recently been named to chair the seven-man *Majlis* committee selected to determine the fate of the hostages.) The conference included numerous revolutionary groups from Africa, the Arab world, and Latin America. Among others, the Palestine Liberation Organization, the Rhodesian Patriotic Front, and a revolutionary Saudi group that called for the overthrow of the Saudi royal family, participated. The American press did not show interest in the conference except for the participation of John Thomas of the American Indian Movement, who met with the American hostages.[35]

In March 1980 the *Kayhan* announced that the Iranian government would be promoting various national liberation groups through approximately 1 billion rials in funds.[36] A three-man committee was reportedly established to allocate these funds to prospective recipients, including the Palestine Liberation Organization, the Philippine Islamic Movement, the Polisario Front in North Africa, certain Lebanese Shiah groups, and the Eritrian Liberation Front.

In May 1980 members of Iran's Central Bank's Foreign Exchange Department allegedly gave the press a list of approximately forty hardline clerics identified as transferring two-thirds of a billion dollars out of Iran.[37] Ayatollah Beheshti, the head of the Islamic Republican Party, was at the top of the list, supposedly transferring 5.6 billion rials (about $80 million). Among others named were Ayatollah Montazeri, Hojatoleslam Rafsanjani, Hojatoleslam Ghaffari, Ali Khamenehi, and Mostafa Chamran. Many transfers were made to Islamic groups, such as the Shiahs in Lebanon, and national liberation groups. Such transfers would suggest that the hardline Islamic clergy not only controls large sums of money, but is actively and covertly promoting revolution in other areas.

Eclectic Philosophy of Revolution

Iran's revolution has included a multiplicity of groups that have published tons of revolutionary literature, but the writings and teachings of two individuals, Ayatollah Khomeini and Dr. Ali Shariati, have proved to be preeminent. Ayatollah Khomeini's teaching has emphasized the "uplifting of the 'down-trodden' (mustaz'afeen)"[38] and has been especially popular among the masses. Dr. Shariati[39] drew from the philosophy of Frantz Fanon, expecially Fanon's *Les damns de la terre* (*The Wretched of the Earth*) that he translated into Persian. Dr. Shariati focused upon oppression and was vehemently opposed to all aspects of colonialism and imperialism, as was Khomeini. Both Ayatollah Khomeini and Dr. Ali Shariati were uncompromising in their approach to what they saw as Western imperialism, and both called for revolutionary change through Islam. Both were also anti-communist.

While Islam represents the primary vehicle of the Iranian revolution, the revolutionary philosophy is eclectic. It draws from the Islamic precepts of justice and concern for the well-being of the poor, but is also anti-imperialist in character and promotes the interests of the oppressed. Its appeal is to everyone that feels oppressed, and could easily extend to Sunnis, particularly if they believe their governments to be corrupt or under the control of Western imperialism. In fact, it has an appeal to oppressed peoples everywhere.

PARAMETERS OF IRANIAN POLICY

As the "private citizens" that were calling for the export of revolution in 1979 assume control of the Iranian Government, a new dimension is added to their earlier revolutionary rhetoric. Both the emergence of an eclectic philosophy of revolution with a broad appeal and the naming of Ayatollah Montazeri as the probable successor of Ayatollah Khomeini suggest that Iran is rapidly assuming the role of a destabilizer in the Gulf, the role of a revolutionary state.

The implications of Iran's actively pursuing the role of a revolutionary state are many when juxtaposed to the underlying political conflicts and external influences in the region. First, Iran will continue its struggle against imperialism as it has in the past, but to a far greater degree. Whereas Iran's interest in opposing any superpower military presence in the Persian Gulf has paralleled that of other Gulf states, Iran is now likely to be more critical of economic relationships and arms transfers that link individual regimes with "imperialism". President Bani-Sadr's assertion that the governments of neighboring states were "not fully independent and subservient to the United States"[40] is a clue to what is to come. Second the conflict between Arab nationalism and Iranian nationalism will be played down in an effort to make Iran's Islamic revolution more appealing to Sunni Arabs as well as to Shiahs. Iran will accordingly emphasize the pan-Islamic nature of its revolution. Iran is likely to take the lead in combatting Zionism and will probably compete with Arab states in an effort to be seen as the most anti-Zionist. In this regard, a sense of Islamic nationalism acting against Zionism would be projected. Third, the conflict between traditionalism and revolution would see Iran actively seeking the overthrow of the traditional Arab governments in the Gulf and the Saddam Hussein regime in Iraq. With approximately 50,000 Iranians participating in the Hajj each year, it seems likely that there will be increased difficulty for the royal family in Saudi Arabia as the Iranians preach revolution. Not only will corruption and high living of the royal family be targeted by Iran, but accusations of wasting natural resources for the benefit of imperialists and the privileged will continue.[41] Fourth, the territorial disputes will persist. Iran's uncompromising approach to negotiations will not be conducive to settling longstanding claims. This would be especially true of Iran's disputes with Iraq. Moreover, it is possible that Iran's claim to Bahrain will reemerge. Some clerics raised this possibility during the fall of 1979.

Relations with the United States and the Soviet Union should continue to be cool. Iran's historic fear of a Soviet invasion would prevent Iran from becoming very close to any Soviet regime. Concerning relations with the United States, Iran will probably move to resolve the hostage crisis, because the fundamentalist clerics are now firmly in power and no longer need the use of the hostages against the religious-based nationalists. The Islamic emphasis on mercy might serve as a possible basis for a hostage release. Anti-American rhetoric is likely to continue, but some trade with the United States should return after the hostage issue is settled.

The Arab-Israeli conflict should continue to be most significant and will provide the issues upon which Iran is likely to base much of its foreign policy. Iran will probably use Jerusalem as the focal point for fueling its revolutionary energies. In the past it had been suggested that a million unarmed Moslems march on Jerusalem to reclaim it for Islam. The idea is likely to surface again.

In terms of oil, Iran will continue to sell oil on the world market, but will take its attack on the Saudi and other conservative Gulf regimes into the Organization of Petroleum Exporting Countries to force both higher prices and the use of the oil weapon against Israel and its supporters.

NOTES

1. It should be noted that Ayatollah Khomeini has avoided directly confronting Iran's difficult political problems, such as the hostage issue or the formation of Iran's first Constitutional Government under the Islamic Constitution. Instead, he has granted responsibility to others while offering only general guidelines.
2. This brings to mind the rivalry between Lenin and Trotsky.
3. For a more comprehensive examination of the Persian Gulf context, see Charles G. MacDonald, *Iran, Saudi Arabia, and the Law of the Sea: Political Interaction and Legal Development in the Persian Gulf* (Westport, Connecticut: Greenwood Press, 1980), pp. 25-58.
4. For background, see Rouhollah K. Ramazani, *The Foreign Policy of Iran: A Developing Nation in World Affairs 1500-1941* (Charlottesville, Virginia: University Press of Virginia, 1966), pp. 92-93.
5. For the text of the treaty, see Nasrollah S. Fatemi, *Diplomatic History of Iran, 1917-1923* (New York: Russel F. Moore, 1952), pp. 317-325.
6. For a discussion of the Anglo-Russian invasion, see Rouhollah K. Ramazani, *Iran's Foreign Policy 1941-1973: A Study of Foreign Policy in Modernizing Nations* (Charlottesville, Virginia: University Press of Virginia, 1975), pp. 30-39.
7. *Ibid.*, pp. 138-139. For Truman's own discussion of his pressure on the Soviets, see *New York Times*, 25 August 1957, p. 1.
8. For a discussion of Khomeini's government-imposed exile, see Marvin Zonis, *The Political Elite of Iran* (Princeton: Princeton University Press, 1971), pp. 44-46.
9. *Ibid.*, p. 46.
10. *Iran Times*, 2 November 1979, p. 14. Khomeini similarly stated, "We are inheritors of a realm which over a period of some 50 years has languished under the pressure of the United States and Britain and of the other superpowers and has turned into a ruin wherein everything is backward and, above all, its manpower is backward." *Iran Times*, 9 November 1979, p. 17.
11. The list was in response to the letter of 187 American Congressmen. For details, see *Iran Times*, 19 September 1980, p. 13.
12. For background on the Irano-Arab Cold War and sources on the Arab revolutionary perspective regarding the Persian Gulf, see Rouhollah K. Ramazani, *The Persian Gulf: Iran's Role* (Charlottesville, Virginia: University Press of Virginia, 1972), pp. 33-41.
13. *Ibid.*, pp. 36-37.
14. See "Arabistan: Another Palestine?", *Arab Observer*, 14 February 1966.
15. For a discussion of the offshore boundary agreements that Iran reached with its neighbors, see Charles G. MacDonald, "Iran's Strategic Interests and the Law of the Sea," *Middle East Journal*, 34 (Summer 1980), pp. 302-322.
16. For a comprehensive examination of territorial disputes in the Persian Gulf, see MacDonald, *Iran, Saudi Arabia, and the Law of the Sea*, pp. 33-37.
17. See Jonathan C. Randal, "Iran is Expecting U.S. Military Aid If Soviets Attack," *Washington Post*, 21 March 1980, p. A-34.
18. *Ibid.*
19. For an overview of Iran's internal power struggle after the fall of the Shah, see Charles G. MacDonald, "Iran: Political and Security Assessment," in *Business and the Middle East: Threats and Prospects*, ed. by Yonah Alexander and Robert A. Kilmarx (Elmsford, New York: Pergamon, forthcoming).
20. For an analysis of Iran's Constitution, see MacDonald, "Iran: Political and Security Assessment."
21. *Iran Times*, 21 September 1979, p. 14.
22. *Ibid.*
23. *Ibid.* See also, *Arab News* (Jeddah), 18 September 1979, p. 3.
24. *Iran Times*, 21 September 1979, p. 14.

25. *Ibid.*
26. *Iran Times,* 12 October 1979, p. 13.
27. *Ibid.*
28. *Ibid.*
29. *Ibid.*
30. *Iran Times,* 16 November 1979, p. 18.
31. See Youssef M. Ibrahim, "New Data Link Mecca Takeover with Islamic Political Discontent," *New York Times,* 25 February 1980, p. A-1.
32. *Iran Times,* 12 October 1979, p. 14.
33. *Ibid.*
34. *Ibid.*
35. For example, see *Christian Science Monitor,* 21 January 1980, p. 5.
36. *Iran Times,* 28 March 1980, p. 14.
37. *Iran Times,* 16 May 1980, p. 16.
38. Rouhollah K. Ramazani, "Iran's Revolution: Patterns, Problems and Prospects," *International Affairs* (London), (Summer 1980), p. 446.
39. Dr. Ali Shariati died under unusual circumstances in England in June 1977. For a biographical sketch of his life, see Shahrough Akhavi, *Religion and Politics in Contemporary Iran: Clergy-State Relations in the Pahlavi Period* (Albany: State University of New York Press, 1980), pp. 144-145.
40. For President Bani-Sadr's comments, see *New York Times,* 29 March 1980, p. C-12.
41. In October 1980 Ayatollah Khomeini emphasized in a speech to a group of ambassadors from Muslim states that Iran sought to convert the governments of Muslim states to the "Islamic outlook that he espouses." He stated the following: "What we want for all countries and all governments is what has happened here—the awakening that occurred in Iran, the distance this puts between the people and the superpowers, the way we cut their hands from our resources. . . You are giving away the wealth of the Muslims—those things that should be used in the interest of the Muslims—to non-Muslims. And for nothing. This was also the case under the deposed Shah, where money used to be poured into America's pocket for their own purposes. . ." *Iran Times,* 31 October 1980, p. 14.

IV. THE AYATOLLAH REVOLUTION: LACK OF CONSENSUS ON FUNDAMENTALS

Enver M. Koury

Like numerous Middle Eastern and Islamic countries, Iran is characterized by complex social diversity. The Ayatollah Revolution was the manifestation of a "mosaic puzzle" because of the plethora of causal determinants. It reflected public demands for Iranian independence from external control, centralization of governmental authority, popular participation, and socioeconomic modernization; as well as public ambivalence toward national integration of the diverse ethnic, communal, and linguistic groups into a homogeneous entity. No single determinant, such as mosaic communal structure, was responsible for the overthrow of the shah. Rather, the communal system was one variable of the complex linkages of the Revolution.

The Ayatollah Revolution did more than put an end to the Pahlavi dynasty. It loosened the grip of the central authority of the government. The disparate ethnic communes that make up at least half of Iran's population welcomed the Revolution both to end the reign of the shah and to share power with the Persian-speaking Iranians. In the words of George Ball:

> With religious leaders in the vanguard, all who hated the shah for quite disparate reasons found a respectable point of unity in the ayatollah's campaign—and in the process discovered with surprise that their anti-Pahlavi sentiments were universally shared.
>
> United only by a common desire to dethrone the shah, the masses marching under Khomeini's flag of convenience were bound to fragment once they had achieved their initial goal, thus precipitating an almost inevitable struggle for power.[1]

Deep communal division is now threatening Iran with civil strife and possible disintegration. The general Islamic movement that toppled the shah is in a state of change in terms of its demands and goals. This chapter will address the regional struggles which may signal a new phase in the Ayatollah Revolution, based on communal self-interest.

Communal identity involves the conscious association of individuals with a specific group, differentiated from other groups. Conflict with the central authority is one means of promoting communal integration; it helps establish identity and reinforces communal solidarity. In addition to serving the function of solidarity, however, communal identity often generates intergroup hostility, as seen in the tension between *ingroup* (e.g., Persian-speaking Iranians or Khomeini regime) versus *outgroups* (e.g., Kurdish and Arab communes) or the *haves* versus the *have-nots*. Iranian intergroup conflict is the result of differences in social stratification systems such as education, economics, and politics; and in cultural beliefs, norms, customs, and values.

Other components of Iranian society, such as middle class pressure, also contribute to the rapidly developing internal conflict. One premise is that the existing crisis is largely ethnoreligious in nature, and arises from opposing power groups pursuing goals that are, or appear to be, incompatable. The opponents are responsible for generating stimuli from the environment, extracting information through their perceptual processes, and then responding to the issues that are blocking their goals. For example, the *sender* (e.g., the central authority) gathers and translates the information into an encoded message, which is then transmitted to the *receiver* (e.g., communal authority) as a signal. Once the signal is received, it becomes a stimulus and then is decoded; that is, extracted and interpreted. When decoded, the receiver responds by encoding his message and returns the signal to the original sender. This interaction between the opposed participants—which can further escalate conflict and hostility-continues through cycles until the issue is solved by one means or another.

The combined effect of the Ayatollah Revolution raises a number of fundamental problems: Is Iran a mosaic or a pluralistic society? Can the existing regime modify some elements of its political posture in an effort to accommodate the mounting demands of the people and the communes? Can the Khomeini regime survive if public support erodes even more than it did under the Shah's regime? These basic problems are the focus of this study and will be approached through an analysis of the following peculiarities of Iranian society:

1. Composition of Iranian society.
2. Primordial leadership and conflicting community interests.
3. Decisionmaking: centralization versus decentralization.

THE COMPOSITION OF IRANIAN SOCIETY

Iran is a heterogeneous country which more closely resembles a mosaic rather than a pluralistic social system. There is probably no definition that adequately captures the complexity of either system. As used here, the distinction between the two is made on a continuum of a heterogeneous frame of reference. The commonalities between mosaic and pluralistic societies include the following: (1) both are of heterogeneous composition with regard to ethnic, linguistic, and/or religious backgrounds; and (2) a variation of the checks-and-balances principle is maintained among the various communities within the society. More important, however, are the differences between mosaic and pluralistic systems on the following issues: (a) general agreement on fundamental cultural values; (b) allocation of power and rewards within the system; and (c) relation of the diverse communities with the central authority. A pluralistic system seems to strike more of a balance between these elements than a mosaic society. The implication is that the tensions in a mosaic system are more enduring and require more ingenuity and more immediate treatment than those in a pluralistic system.

Lack of Central Cultural Values. Political integration and socialization exist in all societies but appear in differing combinations and intensities. In order for a society to mitigate and tolerate internal conflict, strong consensus among the various communities is needed on central cultural values. In analyzing the mosaic structure of Iranian society, the fact must be emphasized that there is a fundamental dichotomy between two sets of central cultural values: (1) national and (2) communal identity. This dichotomy is based on the fact that each ethnic group has its own respective communal identity: that identity requires an exclusion of other communities. Differences among the various Iranian communities are extensive and persistent, thus strengthening communal identity at the expense of national identity.

The concept of community can be better understood if a further distinction is made between the ideas of political community and sense of community. Political community is defined here as a legal-political entity; that is, Iran is a sovereign state over a designated territory. Sense of community, on the other hand, is synonymous with an idea of nation, often extending beyond the border of one or more legal states and encompassing as a cultural entity people with a common history, tradition, and experience, regardless of geographic location. The Kurds, for example, are a tribal-nation, even though they domiciled in several countries—Iraq, Iran, Syria, Turkey, and the Soviet Union. The reason for Iran's identity as a state, but not a nation, is not difficult to understand. Iranian society is a heterogeneous entity, an amlgamation of communities (e.g., Kurds, Persians, and Baluchis), in which the state's authority is still rudimentary and very fragile. The crucial task facing the Khomeini regime is the consolidation of Iran's collection of communal-nations into a viable political community of state—where the sense of national community can prevail over that of the ethnic political community.

The lack of strong central cultural values in Iran cannot be properly appreciated without recognizing the relationship between central values and the process of political socialization and integration. The intricate pattern of Iranian mosaic culture calls simultaneously for two forms of competing political processes. On the one hand, there is a process of national socialization that tends to perform as integrative role in the whole society. On the other hand, Iranian culture equally nurtures communal socialization that produces a disintegrative effect at the national level. Multi-cultural variations, which are based predominantly on different sectarian, ethnic, and kinship values, as well as geographic locales, induce different reactions by the various communes.

Geographical Concentration of Different Ethnic Communities. The present chaotic situation under the revolutionary regime is due partially to the lack of national consensus and partially to the absence of viable sociopolitical integration. These factors are further aggravated by geographic considerations. Communal concentration in certain geographical locales and area imbalances in the distribution of power and rewards present formidable obstacles to the development of viable central cultural values. As shown in Table 1, the lack of balance is most obvious in the ethnic, demographic, geographic, and religious composition of Iran. The lack of national identity (i.e., discongruency) has generated a form of deviant political behavior among sub-groups vis-a-vis the central authority, which is thus delegitimized and drained of support, particularly in time of political crisis.

Within the Iranian mosaic, the various ethnic communes control specific geographical areas of the country. Perhaps more than in any other Middle Eastern country all major ethnic groups in Iran are geographically cohesive. Of the country's minorities, eight major communities are geographically located on the perphery of the predominantly Persian center. Moving counter-clockwise from the north, the eight major ethnic groups are: (1) the Turkomans, (2) the Azerbaijanis, (3) the Kurds, (4) the Lurs, (5) the Bakhtiaris, (6) the Arabs, (7) the Qashqais, and (8) the Baluchis. These communes are of two categories, as shown in tables 2, 3, 4, and 5: those who have common ethnic and language identities and borderlands with neighboring countries—Arabs, Azerbaijanis, Baluchis, Kurds, and Turkomans; and those who are Persian but culturally, and to some extent linguistically distinct—Bakhtiaris, Lurs, and Qashqais.

In the history of the Iranian state, the minority nations have, by virtue of their existence, promoted disintegration of the governmental structure, whenever the central authority has been weakened. The Iranian Arabs, Azerbaijanis, Baluchis, and Kurds have always been troublesome to the Iranian central authority, which has had to fight costly wars with separatist movements in order to hold the country together. Powerful communal sentiments have frequently promoted a decentralizing tendency toward autonomy or secession, and have often been exploited in regional conflicts. The ethnic communes of the border areas are vulnerable to manipulation by neighboring countries:[2] Arabs in the oil-rich Khuzistan province bordering Iraq; Azerbaijanis and Turkomans on the Soviet border; Baluchis on the borders of Afghanistan and Pakistan; and Kurds on the Iraqi, Turkish, and Soviet borders.

The formation of the mosaic character of Iran is partly the manifestation of area geopolitics. The divide-and-rule policy of Great Britain, and other imperialistic powers, drew colonial boundaries in the Middle East with little consideration for ethnic, cultural, linguistic, sectarian, and tribal identities. One such tribal-nation straddling a vast area of several countries is Greater Baluchistan. The Baluchis live in the borderlands of the south eastern fringe of Iran, the southern tier of Afghanistan, and the south western part of Pakistan—an area of 207 thousand square miles extending from the Indus River in Pakistan to the Arabian Sea of west Iran. This area is about twice the size of Arizona.[3]

For nearly a century, a Baluchi political entity existed in the form of a loose federation, a tributary of Afghanistan. However, when Great Britain arrived on the scene in the nineteenth century, Greater Baluchistan was partitioned by the British map-makers. The British gave roughly one-third of the far western part of the federation to Persia (Iran); a small strip in the north became part of Afghanistan. The rest was divided into two parts: one became a puppet principality of Kalat and the other became British India. Following the British withdrawal from India in August 1947, the Kalat principality and British Baluchistan became part of newly independent Pakistan.

The Baluchis, originally from the southern shores of the Caspian Sea, are ethnic kin of the Kurds and have a strong sense of communal socialization and cultural distinctiveness. They are a rugged people, living in

TABLE 1
COMPOSITION OF THE IRANIAN SOCIAL SYSTEM

Community	Language	Religious Sect	Ethnic Group	Population (million)	Kin Location
Arab	Arabic	Shi'ite	Arab	2-3	Iraq
Azerbaijani	Turkish (Azeri)	Shi'ite	Turkish (Azeri)	8-10	U.S.S.R.
Bakhtiari	Luri	Shi'ite	Persian	0.85	
Baluchi	Baluchi	Sunnite		.6-1.2	Afghanistan & Pakistan
Kurd	Kurdi	Sunnite	Kurdish	4-6	Iraq, Syria & Turkey
Lur	Luri			2.5	
Qashqai	Turkic	Shi'ite		0.5	
Turkoman	Turkmeni	Sunnite	Mongol	0.45	U.S.S.R.
Mazanderani				1.5	
Iranian	Farsi	Shi'ite	Persian	17.5	

*Estimates of ethnic population range widely. The uncertainty stems from the various governments' refusal (or possibly the lack of) to publish census data on the ehtnic breakdown of their respective countries' populations. Depending on the circumstances, there is a deliberate tendency to either overstate or understate the size of the various minorities.

TABLE 2
ESTIMATES OF KURDISH POPULATION IN "KURDISTAN"

Country	Minimum	Maximum
Iran	4,000,000	6,000,000
Turkey	7,000,000	12,000,000
Iraq	2,000,000	3,000,000
USSR	.600,000	1,000,000
Syria	.500,000	.600,000
Total	14,000,000	22,600,000

Source: The Middle East, No. 55 (May 1979), p. 52.

TABLE 3
ESTIMATES OF AZERBAIJANI POPULATION IN "AZERBAIJANISTAN"

Country	Minimum	Maximum
Iran	8,000,000	10,000,000
USSR	4,380,000	5.200,000

TABLE 4
ESTIMATES OF BALUCHI POPULATION IN "BALUCHISTAN"

Country	Minimum	Maximum
Iran	.600,000	1,200,000
Pakistan	1,200,000	2,00,000
Afghanistan	.300,000	.600,000

TABLE 5
ESTIMATES OF TURKOMAN POPULATION IN "TURKMENIYA"

Country	Minimum	Maximum
Iran	.100,000	.500,000
USSR	1,000,000	1,500,000

MAP–1
GEOGRAPHIC CONCENTRATION OF ETHNIC MINORITIES

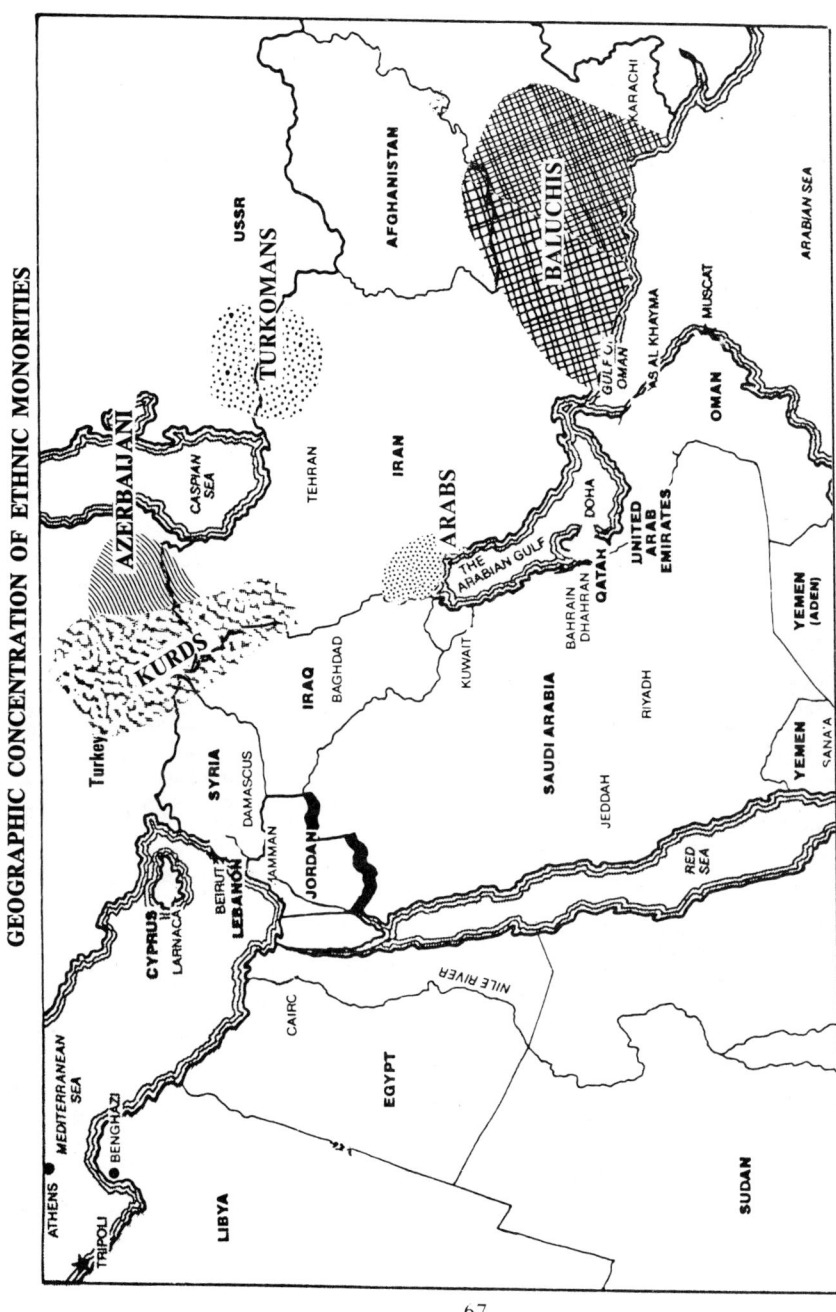

one of the most unattractive and desolate landscapes on earth, characterized by inaccessible mountains and arid desert. The geographic isolation is complemented by ethno-sectarian and linguistic distinctions that have caused trouble for both Iran and Pakistan. The Baluchis feel that their traditional homeland has been colonized. In Iran, the central authority has done very little to encourage a Baluchi intelligentsia or to open the area to the outside world. For their part, the Baluchis have long cherished the notion of a Greater Baluchistan. Tribal leaders continue to shuttle back and forth across the Iranian-Pakistani border to rally their followers behind the separate state idea. From 1972 to 1978, there were numerous Baluchi revolts against Pakistan which were suppressed by military forces and equipment borrowed from the shah of Iran.

As the Baluchis, the Kurds have their own ethnic, sectarian, and linguistic distinctiveness. Geographically, the estimated 14 to 20 million Kurds are spread out in an unequal, but descending, order in contiguous communities. Greater Kurdistan consists of the mountainous areas of southeast Turkey, northeast Iraq, northeast Syria, the southern part of the Soviet Union, and southwest Iran. While still tribal, the fiercely independent Kurds are more cohesive than the Baluchis. For nearly a century, the Kurds have been rising in uncoordinated revolts, only to be suppressed by various central authorities. Supported by the Soviet Union, the so-called Mahabad Republic of Kurdistan was proclaimed in 1946, only to be crushed by the shah's army after eleven months.[4] But Kurdish separatist aspirations have persisted, and the people's hope for a Greater Kurdistan continues to be reflected in the regional instability and internal turmoil in Iran.[5]

Schism Between Shi'ite and Sunnite Moslems. The fragility of the Iranian mosaic is greatly aggravated by its various sectarian communities.[6] Despite modern communication facilities, sectarian identities remain relatively strong. This is due, partly, to the fact that the overwhelming majority of the people in certain geographical locales are of the same sectarian affiliation, especially in areas that are remote from urban centers. Iran's non-Moslem communities constitute perhaps 3 percent of the total population of the country.[7] The Bahais, Christians, and Jews, who live mostly in urban centers of the country, keep an understandably low profile, and are of no threat to the central authority. However, it is the Sunnite minority, constituting about 15 percent of the Moslem population, that is pushing for long-denied minority rights. They may become the most alarming internal force for the Islamic Republic.

The Iranian mosaic is further undermined by the non-separation of religion and state. The adoption of the Shi'ite sect as the state religion was legalized by the new constitution enacted in a referendum in December 1979 and has served to widen the gulf between the two Islamic sects. Disappointment with the new constitution is widespread among the followers of the Sunnite sect. They feel the constitution does not deal adequately with the problem of sectarian rights, as shown in Articles 12 and 19. Article 19 states that: "The people of Iran regardless of ethnic and tribal origin enjoy equal rights. Color, race, language and the like will not be cause for privileges."[8] Article 12, on the other hand, states that: "The official religion of Iran is Islam, and the sect followed is Twelver Shi'ism (Ithna 'Ashari). This principle is never subject to change. Other Islamic denominations also . . . enjoy complete respect. . ."[9] Article 12 clearly makes Islam of the *Jaafari* (i.e., Twelver Shi'ism) the official religion of Iran, even though other Islamic sects are valid and respected. The two articles are bound to affect communal relationships, and any move away from a mosaic and toward a pluralistic system would be in vain.

Khomeini, whose brand of Islamic nationalism united the diverse country against the shah, is now beset with increasing sectarian dissension. One of the most important cohesive components of communal ethnocentrism is the concept of sectarianism. Islamic sects are influential agents of communal socialization, and often have a profound effect on human behavior. In Iran, the ethnic Baluchis, Kurds, Qashqais, and Turkomans, who have their own languages and cultures, are all Sunnite Moslems. Together, they compose about 15 percent of the Moslem population. In the past, their quasi-independence kept them relatively free of both the central authority and the Shi'ite hierarchy. However, the institutionalization of the Shi'ite sect as the official religion of the country could only serve to promote Shi'ite special interests and to encourage ethnic and sectarian anarchy. It is this communal complex-web (i.e., ethnic linguistic-sectarian-geographic integrant) that could become the most disintegrative factor in Iranian society. The situation is further complicated by the fact that the Iranian Sunnite communes have been cushioned by the influence of the Sunnite hierarchy of the entire Moslem world.

Of equal weight is the demographic factor. About 30 percent of the Iranians (e.g., Azerbaijanis, Turkomans, and Qashqais) speak one of the Turkish languages. When they are considered with the other country's linguistic groups (such as the Arabs, Kurds and Baluchis), linguistic minorities "probably come close to equaling the Persian-speaking population of the Iranian heartland."[10] None of these communal minorities has reason to support the new constitution; and the festering sense of discrimination makes them willing participants in the fight to overthrow the Khomeini regime. Consequently, there is every reason to believe that contacts between and among the leaders of the various communes are taking place discreetly.[11] If communal linkages become strong enough, the political breakup of Iran will probably follow.

Iran has a long and often combative history. This is partly due to the fact that Iran has frequently been confronted with both separatist and autonomous sentiment among its communal minorities. Each of the eight major communities has a history of resisting central authority. "Iran's geopolitical situation is so sensitive that [the central authority] cannot permit such disintegration or the threat of civil war."[12] Apprehension about the dissolution of the state is realistic in view of the fact that collectively these major communes constitute about one-third of the area of Iran and encompass the rich agricultural area of Azerbaijan, the huge oil reserves of the Arab-Khuzistan province, and the strategic Hormuz Straits off Baluchistan.

One of the most important factors in Iranian instability is that of communal deprivation. The degree of communal deprivation varies according to the proximity of the various communes to the center of power. Iranian society can be roughly divided into four concentric circles: (1) a decision-making nucleus, which is almost exclusively restricted to those of Persian stock; (2) a center, which is composed mainly of indigenous Persians, and to a lesser extent, Azerbaijanis; (3) a periphery, which is constituted mainly of communes such as Azerbaijanis, Bakhtiaris, and Lurs; and (4) an extreme periphery, which is almost exclusively comprised of Arabs, Baluchis, Kurds, and Turkomans.

By extending a line from the nucleus to the extreme periphery, a continuum of political and socioeconomic positions of the various communes can be demonstrated. Roughly, those communes inside the nucleus circle have the most rewards and are the most satisfied; those communes on the extreme periphery are the least rewarded and most discontent. Discontent is an outcome of deprivation. As Ted R. Gurr states:

[The] . . . existence of what the observer judges to be abject poverty of "absolute deprivation" is not necessarily thought to be unjust or unremediable by those who experience it. As Runciman puts it, "If people have no reason to expect or hope for more than they can achieve, they will be less discontented with what they have, or even grateful simply to be able to hold on to it."[13]

Discontentment arises not so much from *absolute* deprivation, but more as a result of a *relative* deprivation. Relative deprivation among communes in the peripheries is linked to a perception theme of a discrepancy between what those communes feel they are entitled to and what they are actually allotted, especially in comparison with those groups in the nucleus and center circles. The Arabs, Kurds, and Baluchis, for example, use the Persian commune as a point of reference to compare their own unequal share of wealth and their living conditions. Such perceptions have been largely responsible for accelerating tension, conflict, and uprising by the deprived minorities of Iran. Again, ethnocentrism seems to influence this tense situation. There is considerable evidence that a state of imbalance exists, and communal uprising is a clear attempt to bring the structures of the society into equilibrium.

PRIMORDIAL LEADERSHIP AND CONFLICTING COMMUNAL INTERESTS

Another pertinent factor in the Iranian mosaic is the role of primordial leadership. Primordial leadership groupings form a complex-web of the ecclesiastical hierarchy, such as the *mullah* system of the Islamic Shi'ite sect; the boss parties, which are organized by, or closely associated with, religious and/or ethnic communes; and the secularist political parties, such as the Communist Tudeh party. Within this complex-web, the ecclesiastical hierarchy is by far the dominant one. In the words of James A. Bill:

In Iran, the descendants of Ali (the cousin and son-in-law of the Prophet Mohammed) represent a chain of charismatic leaders (Imams), the twelfth of whom went into occultation in A.D. 940. The Shi'ite leaders today, known as "mujtahids," are representatives of this last Iman and wield great spiritual as well as economic and political power. Since 1501 when Twelver Shi'ism became the state religion of Iran, the secular shahs have ruled partially in the shadow of the mujtahids. Iran has been the scene of tension between the secular and religious leaders ever since.[14]

Structurally, the Shi'ite ecclesiastical hierarchy is pyramidal. At the bottom of the pyramid are the *mullahs,* whose estimated number is about 180,000—"roughly one for every 200 persons in the population. . . Those who carry their studies further. . . acquire the title 'Hafez' (the memoriser). There are at least 100,000 such persons. Above them are those who.. acquire the title 'hojjat'(vicar)."[15] It is from this group that some individuals move up in the rank to become *mujtahids* (interpreters; that is possessing the right to pass judgements). "From this. . . hierarchy there emerges a small group of especially learned and respected clergy who by a form of popular acclaim acquire the title 'ayatollah'. . ." [16] At the top of the pyramid, there are the very few *Al-Ozma* (Grand) Ayatollahs, "whose number could vary between six and ten although there is no limit,"[17] and who form a sort of supreme council. As of 1980, its members include: (1) Ruhollah Khomeini, (2) Kazem Shariat-Madari, (3) Abul-Ghassem Khoyin Najaf, (4) Muhammad Reza Golpayagani, (5) Marashi-Najafi, and (6) Hossein Khonsari. All live in Qom, except Khoy and Khonsari, who reside in Tehran.

Ecclesiastical hierarchies, especially those of the Shi'ite sect, are far better organized than either the boss or the secularist political parties. Functionally, the mosque is still an integral part of the life of the ordinary individual and serves as a place for disseminating information among the followers in a relatively effective communication service. Since they are close to popular feeling and needs, the *mullahs* serve as social and economic welfare agents throughout the country, and consequently their views have an aura of legitimacy.[18]

The impotence of national political associations (i.e., blocs, fronts, and parties) has led to outright conflict, often quite violent, because primordial ties (ethnic, sectarian, linguistic, kinship, and fealty identities) still constitute the basic configurations of the political process. Aside from their proclaimed principles or goals, none of these primordial associations is nationally based or integrative and representative of the nation as a whole. Such associations are, with very few exceptions, closely identified with parochial and personal rivalries, which in a time of crisis can easily engender social disintegration. Lacking structural organization, no political association can gain political advantage without the support of the ecclesiastical hierarchy. But combined with ecclesiastical authority, they could easily manipulate the masses and advance their respective interests. In case of conflict, however, the balance of power usually tilts in favor of the ecclesiastic hierarchy.

The political associations at work in Iran today do not neatly fit the broad patterns of a particular political ideology or orientation, such as reactionary, conservative, liberal, or radical. Rather, the tendency is toward a rough spectrum with a more sectarian pole opposed to a more secular pole. At one extreme of the spectrum, there are those who adhere to fundamentalist Islam; at the other extreme, are those who subscribe to a Marxist secular outlook. Between these two extreme mental postures there are many shades of political outlooks which cut across national movements and communal sects.

At one end of the political spectrum, there is first the extreme right-wing Islamic Republican Party (IRP–*Hizbie Jomhourie Islami*). It is supported by the pro-Khomeini clergy faction and aims to establish itself as the single party of Iran with the slogan of: "There is no party but the party of Allah." In opposition to or competition with the Islamic Republican Party is the moderate right-wing Moslem People's Republican Party (MPRP–Islamic Republic of Kalgh Mussalman Party). It has strong roots in the Azerbaijan region, the home of Iran's largest minority, with strong loyalty to Ayatollah Kazem Shariat-Madari, who is an Azerbaijani. The rivalry between these two religious parties is an affirmation that the ecclesiastical leaders do not constitute a monolithic, homogeneous whole.

At the other extreme of the spectrum, the opposition to Khomeini's party comes from leftist forces which are quite radical. These are the Communist Tudeh party, the Marxist *Fedayeen-el-Khalq,* and the Islamic *Mujahedeen-el-Khalq*. The first two fall within the secular/socialist movement, and the third is a form of Islamic socialism. While the political style of the three parties is predominantly ideological, only the Communist Tudeh party is closely associated with the Soviet Union. Its membership is limited to urban centers, especially to the city of Tehran. Both the *Feda-*

yeen and *Mujahedeen* draw their followers from the educated youth and military establishment, with some support from the masses. Both identify their goals more with national interests. The *Fedayeen* is a secularist movement aimed at the destruction of class privilege and foreign tutelage. The *Mujahedeen* is a sectarian movement, aimed at the establishment of a classless society of "pure Shi'ism."[19] Tactically, all three forces seem determined to throw their weight behind groups that undermine Khomeini's power.

At center of the spectrum, there are two nationalist organizations of some influence. The larger one is the right-center National Front that briefly held power in the early 1950's under the leadership of late Prime Minister, Dr. Mohammed Mossadegh. The National Front is a loosely organized grouping, whose leadership—drawn largely from the upper middle class—enjoys the support of educated and professional members of the urban centers, with limited supported from the masses and upper class. The other nationalist organization—which split from the National Front—is the left-center National Democratic Front, led by Dr. Hedayat Matin-Daftary, the grandson of the late nationalist Dr. Mossadegh. Like other forces to the left, the National Democratic Front has shown courage in criticizing the Khomeini regime and the fundamentalist approach of "the Grand Ayatollah".

There are also communal political associations whose identities center around clanism, ethnism, and sectarianism. The disintegrative tendencies of these associations expressed in a push for communal autonomy and secession, threaten national unity. The least organized of the communal groups are the Baluchis in the southeast and the Turkomans in the northeast. In Khuzistan, the key oil-producing region, the Iranian Arab opposition is concentrated around the Arab Ayatollah Taher Shobeir Khaqani. The Kurdish political associations also have a religious base, for the Kurds, like the Baluchis and Turkomans, are mostly Sunnite Moslem. (The Azerbaijanis, Iranian Arabs, and Persians are predominately of the Shi'ite sect.) The main opposition to the Khomeini regime includes four major groups. The Kurdish Democratic Party Provisional Leadership (KDP-PL) is led by Massoud, the younger son of the late *Mullah* Mustafa Barzani. The Kurdistan Democratic Party (KDP) is composed of two wings: one is based in Iraq and the other in Iran, under the leadership of Abdar-Rahman Ghassemlou. The third faction is the Union of Kurdish Nationalists (UKN). The fouth major group, the Iraqi Patriotic Union of Kurdistan (PUK), operates under the leadership of Jalal Talabani.

While these political associations adhere to different programs and ideologies, their perpetuity usually hinges upon the quality of the leaders. Leadership in Iran traditionally "has revolved around personalities, not parties."[20] The associations are esentially appendages of notable and esteemed men. Most of the above-mentioned political associations have their own "heroes." The strength of the Moslem People's Republican Party, for example, is not expressed in its official leader or the party's machine, but in the person of the Grand Ayatollah Shariat-Madari, the Shi'ite religious leader of the Azerbaijani Turks.[21] This explains, in part, why the major strength of this party is concentrated in the Azerbaijani provinces of Iran. The Islamic Republican Party, consisting mainly of Khomeini's followers, derives its power not from the party's cleric founders—Ayatollah Mohammed Beheshti, Akbar Hashemi Rafasanjani, Abd Al-Karim Mousavi, and others—but from Iran's first-ranking religious leader, Grand Ayatollah Khomeini.

The central authority in Iran historically has had little control over powerful communal leaders who often have been able to assert their power within their respective communes. Most ethnic-linguistic-sectarian communes have their own pyramidal power centers and their own communal source of strength. One credible leader, for example, is the Sunnite religious figure, Sheikh Sayed Ezzedin Hussaini, of the province of Kurdistan. The Kurds remain essentially a tribal people, and charismatic religious leadership is vital to the Kurdish political movement. While Dr. Abdar—Rahman Ghassemlou, the head of the Kurdish Democratic Party, is a dynamic leader, "much of the special atmosphere of Kurdistan can be attributed to the influence of . . . Izzedin Hussaini, a 58-year-old Sunni mullah and a most unusual cleric for Iran. He is rapidly becoming recognised as the Iranian Kurds' national leader."[22]

One concept which should be stressed in this analysis is the centrality of leadership. Shi'ite centrism is an ideology or belief that extends into the realm of leadership. "The influence of personality in Iranian politics has always been a matter of paramount importance. When combined with religious charisma, it is all the more so."[23] In extreme cases, the centrality of charismatic leadership tends to elicit uncritically supportive attitudes and submissive outlooks. In Shi'ite theology, there is a theory that the Imamate and Moslem rule are obligatory. Barring the philosophical dispute over whether the Imamate is the responsibility of the people or of God, the supporters of this theory include the Shi'ites. Shi'ites claim that the establishment of the leadership of the Imam and Islamic rule is essential to society, with the object of protecting both the spiritual and material interest of the people. "Central to this is the Messianistic Concept of the 'hidden Imam' the 12th Imam, Hazrat Vali-e-Asr Imam Mehdi—who 'disappeared' in 873-4 A.D. In his absence the community is seen as lacking possibility of legitimate rule, and de facto authority is vested in the *ulema* (theological experts)."[24]

The Messianistic concept of the "hidden Imam" emphasized martyrdom, and Shi'ism allows for the presence of an intermediary or *faghih* (i.e., a religious guardian, in the absence of the "hidden Imam") between God and the people. This messianic cast "was greatly strengthened in the early Nineteenth Century by Agha Muhammad Baqir Bihbihani, who founded the *Usuli* school or tendency. He argued that the community of Moslims could be divided into two groups: *Mojtaheds* (leaders) and their *muallids* (followers.)"[25] As the clerical hierarchy became more institutionalized, the *mullah* leadership concentrated and centralized its power through mass persuasion and public mobilization. They developed a unique Shi'ite political thought, as shown by the constitutional movement at the turn of the twentieth century.

> The Constitution . . . [of 1906] was in many respects a landmark for the Shiia clergy. In 1906 the majority supported the concept of a constitutional monarchy with built-in guarantees on the observance of Islamic principles. The guarantees were based on the formation of a council of five religious elders to act as custodians of Islamic principles. [The elected members of the council **were chosen** by the Assembly from a list of 20 mojtaheds nominated by the **ulema**.] [26]

The schisn. between the Pahlavi dynasty and the Shi'ite ecclesiastical hierarchy developed when Mohammed Reza Shah challenged the authority of the religious leaders. This confrontation eventually led to his overthrow. The Ayatollah Revolution, in essence, reasserted the Islamic principles and leadership in the 1980 Constitution. The constitutional debate "may have more in common with the Nuri-Naini dispute [over the 1906 Constitution] of 70 years ago than with Western conceptions of constitutionalism."[27] The leading exponent of clerical opposition to the 1906 constitutional movement was Ayatollah Fazlollah Nuri whose pretext was the "demand for the full implementation of the *sharia*."[28] The leading clerical advocate of the movement was Ayatollah Mohammad Husain Naini who "argued strongly that the avoidance of tyranny was a religious duty and that the best or most reliable antidotes to tyranny were the principles of election and consultation. [He] further insisted that the role of the *mojtaheds* should be supervisory, not executive."[29]

The debate over the 1980 constitutional movement is centered around three religious factions. The dominant faction—whose members are still a minority—is led by Ayatollah Khomeini, with a position closer to the views of the Ayatollah Nuri. Members of this faction are the reactionary fundamentalists, calling for a full implementation of the *sharia*. The second action represents those who support views reminiscent of Ayatollah Naini and favor a constitution similar to that of 1906. The constitutional approach is based on the principles of election and consultation, and maintains that the role of the religious leaders should be supervisory rather than executive. At one time this faction was centered around Ayatollah Taleghani, but after his death in 1979 the faction has had no recognized leader. The third faction represents the traditionalists, who believe that in the absence of the "hidden Imam", it is impossible to implement the *sharia*. Members of this faction are "led by Ayatollah Shariat-Madari, with their 'quietist' tendency are still in a majority, particularly among the senior clergy."[30] The creation of the new republic reveals the differences in outlook: Should it be an Islamic Republic and reflect Khomeini's outlook of Islamic fundamentalism and purity; or should it be an Islamic Democratic Republic and reflect Shariat Madari's desire to blend the religious and national principles into a pragmatic unity?

In the messianistic concept of the "hidden Imam" leaders are not really elected; they just emerge. The notion of popular acceptance is not based on an election principle. The original draft of the 1980 Constitution, for example, proposed an elected presidential system with a Goliath at the top of the pyramid and a rubber stamp type of Majlis (i.e., National Assembly). After the death of Ayatollah Taleghani, however, the Khomeini faction was able to add to the first draft the office of *velayat faghih* (i.e., religious trustee, guardian or leader) above that of an elected president. The Constitution provides that a *velayat faghih* will carry the burden of leadership in the continuing absence of the Twelfth Imam (the hidden Imam). To qualify, the leader must be "just, pious, enlightened, courageous, sagacious and competent to manage affairs." While there are no procedures about who the *velayat faghih* will be—a council or just one man—article 107 makes it clear that Ayatollah Khomeini is just such a trustee.[31]

In its preamble, the Constitution represents the ground for the leadership of the clergy.[32] Article 109 also makes it clear that future *faghihs* will be clergymen.[33] Atop the pyramidal structure is a *faghih*—God's representative on earth—with extensive power, as "supreme religious leader of the Islam-based republic."[34] He has the "power to virtually pick the President—in fact the power not only to veto nominations but to veto the result of the election after the event—and also the powers of the Supreme Commander have been invested in this position."[35] Furthermore, the *faghih* has the power to appoint and dismiss the Chief of the General Staff, to set up the National Defense Council, to declare war and make peace on the recommendation of the National Defense Council, and to dismiss the president either on a vote of no confidence by the National Assembly or on the basis of a Supreme Court decision.[36]

Directly below the *faghih* is the Council of Guardians (i.e., the Council for the Protection of the Constitution). It is composed of twelve members—six *mujtahids* (i.e., scholars of Islamic law able to deduce particular applications through the use of independent reasoning), who are appointed by the *faghih*, and six experts in legal matters, who are introduced to the National Consultative Assembly by the High Council of the Judiciary, who are voted on by the Assembly.[37] The task of the Council of Guardians is to safeguard against any deviation from the true Islamic functions and obligations. According to Article 96:

> The majority of the six religious members of the Council of Guardians decides whether a national assembly law is in contradiction with Islamic decrees. And the majority of all the members of the Council of Guardians decides whether a constitutional law is in contradiction with the Islamic decrees.[38]

Beneath the Council of Guardians is the government. Article 57 divides the state power into executive, legislative and judicial bodies.[39] Although the Constitution provides for an elected President and National Consultative Assembly, candidates for the presidency are selected by the Council of Guardians. Sections 4 and 5 of article 110 state that the duties and powers of the *faghih* or members of the Leadership Council are:

> Signing the order [formalizing] the election of the president after he has been elected by the people. Approving the competence of candidates for the presidency with regard to the qualifications specified by this law. Confirming them before the Council of Guardians before the elections and confirming the president's first term.

> Dismissing the president of the republic in consideration of the good of the country after an order is issued by the Supreme Court charging him with violating his legal duties toward the National Consultative Assembly and relieving him of his political competence.[40]

Moreover, the *faghih*, in consultation with the Supreme Court judges, appoints the head of the Supreme Court and the attorney general who are two of the five members of the High Council of the Judiciary.[41] As a result of the introduction of the principles of the *faghih*, Ayatollah Khomeini has very extensive powers. Through his power to appoint half the members of the Council of Guardians and the head of the judicial body, the *faghih* can in fact control the whole process of the government. A constitution that gives practically all powers to one leader (i.e., *faghih*) could easily provoke a battle among all Iranian leaders, including those of the communes.

CRISIS DECISIONMAKING:
CENTRALIZATION VERSUS DECENTRALIZATION

Iran has a history of extensive violence. Iranian policymakers have come to expect it and rationalize its inevitability on the basis of past experience. The process of national integration has always been in a state of precarious balance, and accordingly has been of the highest priority in the minds of the various policymakers. The Azerbaijani-Kurdish crisis of 1945-46, which led to a short period of secession of the two communes, is a constant reminder of possible communal uprising.[42] The 1978-80 agitation of the Arabs, Baluchis, and Turkomans and the uprising of the Azerbaijanis and Kurds pose serious threats to the central authority and require more immediate attention than any other national goal. A power vacuum exists; and when the high expectations of the communes coincide with anomic crisis, action justifying violence is likely to emerge.

As of 1982, Iran is still in the midst of a crisis which can be defined as a set of rapidly unfolding events. The crisis has been an intensive input rapidly fed into both the communal and national political systems, and involves actual and/or potential conflict where decisions become restricted by the threatening situation. Although it is difficult to foresee the outcome of the Ayatollah Revolution, it is very obvious that the seizure of power by the *mullah* forces does not mean the end of the revolution. "It merely ushered in a new phase. . . [and the] underlying problems facing the revolution are numerous."[43] But central to these underlying problems is the perceptual process. According to Dina A. Zinnes' findings: whether hostility actually exists is irrelevant. What is relevant is the perception of hostility, and as long as the involved decisionmakers feel that their country or commune is the target of hostility, they will respond accordingly.[44] Under such circumstances, opposing decisionmakers tend to reveal uniform patterns of perceiving hostility, of experiencing rising frustration, and of escalating violence.

In an attempt to understand the impact and effects of the Ayatollah Revolution, a model is presented in this section to explore social conflict between communal and central authorities and their opposed goals. This model, however, does not account for all the features of the "real world." It offers only partial and approximate explanation, as a way of organizing the situation as perceived by the leaders of the opposing authorities. More specifically, the model emphasizes the role of the decisionmakers as the primary unit of analysis. This approach is based on several circumstances. First, the role of decisionmaker in Iranian intra-politics is extremely crucial in influencing the nation's conflict behavior. Second, as the primary actor in policy formulation, the Iranian policymaker does not operate in a vacuum; rather, he works within larger units of the institutional and societal complex. Third, the perception of the decisionmaker usually reflects the overall perceived environment, which often includes most of the elements that have been previously discussed.

The interactive process of conflict is one of sharing information between the *sender* (e.g., the central authority) and *receiver* (e.g., communal authorities). The process of conflict consists of three basic steps: (1) *stimulus input* (i.e., crisis or event); (2) *perception* (i.e., intervening mental activity); and (3) *response output* (i.e., resultant action or decision). As shown in Diagram 1, the relationship between crisis (i.e., stimulus or

"S") and decision (i.e., response or "R") can be likened to a two-step mediated stimulus-response model—S.r:s.R.—S.r:s.R—where the decisionmaker's perception (r) and statement (s) stand between the stimulus (S) and response (R).[45] Consequently, when crisis occurs, it may be evaluated and perceived by the receiver. The perception (r) of the stimulus (S) is the way the event is described by the decisionmaker. The perception of the receiver eventually leads to a pronouncement (i.e., statement of plans and intentions or "s"), and act (i.e., response or "R") accordingly. In responding the receiver sends a signal (stimulus or "S") back to the original source or sender, who, in turn, responds accordingly.

To appreciate the impact of the Ayatollah Revolution, one must examine the perceptual process by which Iranian decisionmakers receive and extract information about the physical makeup and social setting of their environment. There are two basic components to perception: the cognitive and affective dimensions. Since perception involves receiving and extracting information, it deals partly with the cognitive (i.e., knowledge) tendency. This tendency has two integrants, learning and thinking. Learning can be viewed as the acquisition of knowledge for future reference and thinking as the cognitive aspect of problem solving. Another component of perception is the affective tendency (i.e., the emotional dimension of knowledge) which deals with attitudes and judgements. The affective tendency exists in communal ethnocentrism where sentiment and pride in the commune become the center of everything. The commune itself becomes a frame of reference to rate all others. This notion of stereotype suggests the functional complexity and importance of perception in decisionmaking.

In their reconstructed world, Iranian communal and national policymakers usually assume that what seems just and fair to them is the same for others as well. .This is not the case, for the various communal policymakers often perceive reality in differing ways. In his research, Ole Holsti contends that:

> Decision-makers act upon their definition of the situation and their images of states. . . . These images are in turn dependent upon the decision-maker's belief system, and these may or may not be accurate representations of "reality." Thus. . . conflict frequently is not between states, but rather between distorted images of states.[46]

Policymakers act and react according to their images of the world (i.e., reconstructed situations); the reality of each world is what each policymaker believes it to be. One way to delineate these reconstructed worlds in the present crisis of Iran is to examine how communal and national policymakers perceive the concept of autonomy.

The state of tension between the central and communal authorities can be explained in terms of polarization over the political meaning of autonomy. In an effort to elicit the support of the various Iranian minorities against the shah, Ayatollah Khomeini initially favored a sort of autonomy for the ethnic communes. Following the downfall of the Shah, the Kurds led "other minorities in demanding autonomy in a federated state to be guaranteed in a new constitution."[47] On *Brotherly Unity* and *National Rights*, the Constitution states:

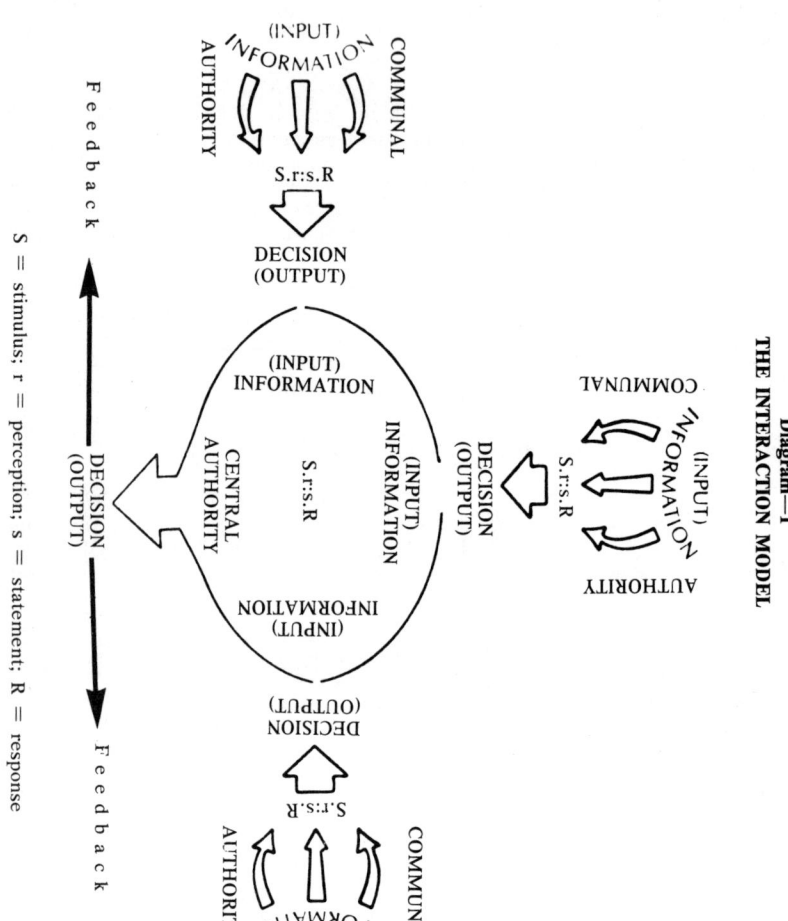

Diagram—1
THE INTERACTION MODEL

S = stimulus; r = perception; s = statement; R = response

1. O ye people, we have created you from a male and a female, and have made you into peoples and tribes that ye might know one another.

2. The noblest of you in the sight of God is he who is most righteous (The Surah of the Inner Apartments).

3. O ye people, since your Lord is one, and since your Father is one, there is no preference for Arab above alien, nor for alien above Arab, nor for black above red, nor for red above black, except in righteousness. (Saying of the Prophet).[48]

> The people of Iran regardless of ethnic and tribal origin enjoy equal rights. Color, race, language, and the like will not be cause for privilege.[49]

The interaction between the adversary leaders can be viewed as a flow of signal between the Stimulus-perception-statement-Response (S.r.s.R) motions linked by feedback processes. The perceptions (r) of the stimuli (S) of the various communal decisionmakers to Khomeini's autonomy (original response--R) were, on the whole, negative. "Leaders of the various national groups opposed the constitution because it did not give them the degree of autonomy they sought."[50] Their actual statements (s) can be summed up in the following manner: The action (R) of Khomeini was "illegitimate" and "imperialistic." It was a policy of communal semicolonization which violated the principle of self-determination and the rights of ethnic minorities. "Nonetheless, the new Baluchi authorities," for example, "feel confident they can end the long record of semicolonial central government discrimination against Baluchistan that has left the province as poor[as]—if not poorer [than]—any in Iran."[51]

Khomeini's statements provoked several responses (R) by the communal decisionmakers. Early reactions (R), for example, were in the form of demonstrations and violent outbursts against the central authority. This was followed by an attempt among some communes to enter into alliances (R) among themselves in an effort to coordinate their activities against the Khomeini regime, and also to secure outside support (R) such as arms. The Iraqi Kurdish "guerrilla leader, Massoud Barzani, . . . had joined the Iranian Kurds with 3,000 of his best fighters."[52] These responses were sent into the environment and served as additional stimuli for the ongoing interactions that link the adversary leaders.

Each of these communal actions (R) served as stimuli (S) to the revolutionary regime. Khomeini's perception (r) of the communal policymakers' attitudes and behavior toward Iran was the mirror image of this contention. Khomeini's refusal to grant autonomy was based on the belief that some ethnic minorities (e.g., Arabs, Kurds, and Baluchis) wanted to be united with their fellow tribesmen in neighboring countries.

> The constitution makes no provision for any deviation from a highly centralized state. This stand reflects a long-held Persian fear that autonomy for Kurdistan could prompt similar demands from oil-rich Khuzestan, Baluchistan, the Turkomans and Azerbaijan, which account for roughly half of Iran's population.[53]

The Ayatollah was of the opinion that some communal leaders were committed to "total separation," with the expressed intention of demolishing the Iranian state. He perceived the opposition's actions (R) as intensely "evil," and an "inhumane" attack on Iran. The opposition leaders were "guilty" of aggressive acts against the sovereignty and integrity of the country.

In response to the challenge to his power, Khomeini defined the events (r) by the opposition's actions, formulated his objectives (s), and consequently reacted (R) by sending his revolutionary guards to put down all forms of opposition (e.g., demonstrations and riots) against his revolutionary regime. Faced with the resulting political and economic difficulties, the regime launched a campaign of discrimination (R) against certain communes (e.g., Kurds and Baluchis). The central government also encouraged rivalry between some communes (e.g., Kurds versus Azerbaijanis) in an attempt to prevent possible communal alliance against the central authority. These threatening actions by Khomeini, in turn, tended to confirm the initial thinking of the communal leaders that their perception of Khomeini's intention was correct. They become more inclined to increase their hostile actions.

Opposing leaders tend to reach different meanings in the ambiguous constitutional articles regarding equal rights. The perception of autonomy can be broadly expressed in the following ways: On the one hand, the communal leaders are arguing for autonomy, with local legislative and judicial, as well as executive powers. On the other hand, Khomeini feels that autonomy must be limited to adminstrative functions. This has been clearly expressed by Abol-Hassan Bani Sadr, the President of the Islamic Republic:

> . . . I agree that the people [Kurds] of that region should administer their own economic and cultural affairs. But they also want to retain control of the police and gendarmerie. Where else in the world is there any autonomy?
>
> If they want autonomy within the framework of Iran it must be within the ideological framework of the Islamic Republic. They must be Muslim. How can we give autonomy within the framework of an Islamic society to those who do not consider themselves bound by Islamic law?
>
> They seem to want a government in which the armed forces are nominally under central control but in practice under their control. They also want the police and gendarmerie to be composed of their own people, but they want a budget from the central government. If they want to retain all affairs in their own hands, why should we give them a budget? This is something other than autonomy. . . I, in the name of the nation, announce that we will not accede to the separation of the single centimetre of Iranian soil.[54]

Certain mental and environmental factors influence the gathering, extraction, and evaluation of information. However, the process by which adversary Iranian leaders gather and perceive information is usually biased, for each leader has his own unique image of any situation. Thoughts about the meaning of autonomy are not only selectively organized by the various communes, but also are clustered in belief systems.

Consequently, important actions emerge, centering on the principle of communal image. Each opposing faction becomes a nucleus around which distinct attitudes, goals, and actions cluster and develop. Violence and legitimacy become almost synonymous in such an environment; and violence is seen as a rightful means for securing communal interests.

WHAT IS THE ALTERNATIVE?

Central-communal interaction consists of two interrelated responses. On the one hand, the central authority (i.e., Khomeini regime) perceives itself to be the object of hostility of the various communes, such as the Kurds and Baluchis; and, in turn, the communes perceive themselves as the object of Khomeini's hostility. Each actor perceives the other as hostile and opportunistic, and each reacts in kind. Taken together, these effects influence the lines of communication (i.e., signals) between the adversary sender and that of the receiver, resulting in increased stress. "As stress increases, decision-makers . . . tend to perceive the range of alternatives open to themselves as becoming narrower."[55] In this state of high stress, the tendency of the Iranian adversaries is to increase their selective perceptions of information, and often they fail to distinguish between the relevant and irrelevant.

As long as there is a power struggle in Iran, the unity of the country will remain in doubt. The ethnic and sectarian fragmentation potential is increased by the socioeconomic difficulties the country faces. All these forces have provided fertile ground for the communal leaders to mount their offensive against the revolutionary regime. As of 1982, the gravity of the crisis in Iran is equidistant between the point of surprise, where adversary decisionmakers are of the notion that hostility is a strong possibility, and the point of no escape, where the same decisionmakers are of the opinion that other alternatives are less and less likely and thus hostility becomes inevitable. The prospect of a prolonged struggle is real, and the future of the country looks decidedly unhealthy.

Reconstruction of the Iranian political system is now a matter of extreme urgency. A strategy of bargaining is needed to mitigate the crisis situation. Such a strategy must include the following suppositions: (1) flexibility in the form of alternative options for peaceful resolution, and a distinction drawn between the possible and the probable; (2) flexibility in the creation of working arrangements to meet basic changes in the situation; and (3) competence to measure the viability of each alternative option and to assess the events from the perspective of the respective parties. In a country in which constitutional engineering must be a fine art, Iran today is faced with at least three alternative courses of action. At opposite ends of the scale are the options of secession and unity. Between these two extremes there is the option of a federal system.

In any civil war, the outcome must be victory for one side or a stalemate. Protracted civil strife in Iran makes it increasingly difficult for both sides to seek a peaceful resolution. Military stalemate seems to be the only means of promoting peaceful resolution. For various reasons, the realization of either of the extreme options, secession or a forced unitary system, appear unfavorable. Although a leaderless and disunited opposition work in Khomeini's favor for now, eventually he will have to confront the reality that his "problems boil down to simple demographics."[56] The

Persian-speaking Iranians of the Shi'ite **sect—who** form Khomeini's main **supporters—make** up 45 percent of the country's population. Even though Shi'ism is still Iran's dominant sect, the ethnic equation of population is in favor of non-Persians—Arabs, Azerbaijanis, Baluchis, Kurds, and Turkomans.

One way to achieve either of the two extreme options (i.e., secession or unitary) is through military force. Communal uprisings represent the greatest threat to the central authority, and it appears that Khomeini has made the crushing of such opposition his top priority. Having committed his prestige to a military effort to crush communal opposition, Khomeini confronts the prospects of a nascent guerrilla war with Iran's many populous minorities. As the secretary general of the Kurdish Democratic Party points out, "there are 100,000 armed Kurdish men who are willing to die for their ideals. [And] we will make Kurdistan the graveyard of the reactionary regime."[57] Already the Kurdish uprising has proven a source of opposition to the central regime. "Without a strong military to counter these local outbreaks. . . . Khomeini will be forced to give in to at least some demands for regional autonomy or face a continuation of antigovernment [unrest] and open the door for opposition leaders."[58]

Some communes have consistently and actively resisted Tehran's centralized control. The loss of Kurdish cities and towns to the national army, for example, represents a setback to the morale of the autonomy-seeking minorities. However, "it is still clear that crushing the Kurds will not be easy and the longer that struggle goes on the more likely it is that other groups will join in the fray."[59] Such a struggle might mark the beginning of a long drawn-out guerrilla campaign against the central authority. Some communes of Iran are rapidly learning the techniques of guerrilla warfare, and have been successful in obtaining arms supplies with antiaircraft batteries and antitank missiles. The armed forces of the central authority may be able to continue routing the guerrillas from cities and towns. However, long, drawn-out guerrilla warfare will prove a major drain on the credibility and resources of the regime.

It was mentioned previously that a military stalemate could open the way toward a political resolution. Nevertheless, if civil strife should be prolonged, the probability of a breakup of the country is real. Conceivably, in prolonged civil strife, the Azerbaijanis could join forces in separatist schemes with the Arabs, Baluchis, Kurds, and Turkomans.[60] An alliance among some communes could be detrimental to Iran for much "of the nation's grain comes from Turkish-speaking Azerbaijan and oil is produced in the ethnic Arab stronghold of Khuzistan province—both areas of regional unrest."[61] Of these communes, the Azerbaijanis could tilt the balance against the central authority. "Not only do they represent more than a third of the population . . , but they are the nation's middle class."[62] There is an Iranian saying that the Azerbaijanis "are like a camel—hard to rouse and get up onto their feet, but once up, hard to stop. So it is that their opposition to the Ayatollah Khomeini began as a protest, turned into a demonstration, then a revolt, and now a challenge to the theocratic regime that Khomeini has just imposed on the nation."[63]

Neither secession nor the unitary approach is a viable means to ensure the interests of Iran. One practical solution for the present crisis would be a communal federal system. While political science offers no universally acceptable guidelines for determining the right formula, the proper mix of a centralized and federal structure along American, West

German, Swiss, or Yugoslav lines is most satisfactory. This proposed communal federal system would be dynamic and stress process and function. It would empower the central authority to handle foreign, defense, banking and major inter-economic projects. Communal or local authorities would be responsible for such things as local security, taxes, economic projects, education (including communal and national languages), and cultural life.

While claims vary, the Kurds' principle demands, for example, include the joint control of military installations in Kurdistan, "an enlarged Kurdish province, a freely elected Kurdish assembly, and recognition of Kurdish as their region's official language."[64] The Baluchi perception of autonomy can also be summed up in the following manner:

> We will give our full support to the [Tehran] government as long as there is no disrespectful behavior toward our [Sunni] religion and our national rights are respected.
>
> Included in national rights. . . were teaching the Sunni rite and the now banned Baluchi language in schools and the "maximum use of local talent" in the province's administration, including the police and military forces stationed here.[65]

Being the largest minority, the Azerbaijanis' demand for autonomy differs from the smaller communes—the Arabs, Turkomans, or Baluchis. "The best educated, most organized, richest and most politicized of Iran's ethnic minorities, Azerbaijanis consider the Persians not as their betters, but as their equals."[66] All communes, however, share the feeling that they are not receiving their fair share of the country's wealth and are determined to challenge the central authority. They all claim that they are not separatists, but want their basic rights.[67]

With the collapse of the ethnically repressive and centralized Pahlavi dynasty and with rise of the weak and far from nationally accepted revolutionary regime, various minorities are pressing their claims for communal autonomy.[68] Except for a few cities, some communes (e.g., Kurds) are acting independently. With some variations, they all demand "self-determination" within the framework of Iran. Most communal leaders favor greater autonomy and deny any separatist aspirations. Shariat-Madari's supporters in the Moslem People's Republican Party predict further civil strife unless Khomeini confers a greater measure of autonomy.[69]

The central authority should realize that Iran's politically estranged communes will not be secured until ethnic groups are given a wider range of local authority and greater participation in the national decisionmaking process. The federal system would embody not only a balance of power among the communes but a balance of power between the communes and the federal authority. The Iranian problems are essentially socioeconomic and political, and military approaches could only play into the hands of the separatists. Policies designed to promote equitable economic development and to moderate the discrimination in the rim lands are essential to the integrative process. And programs such as rural electrification, road-building, and improved communications will better integrate the communal borderlands into the country.

A federal system is the only realistic approach to a viable nation-state comprised, as Iran is, of ethnic, sectarian, and linguistic minorities who, together, constitute over 50 percent of the population. The allocation of power to the communes on the one hand and the federal authority on the other is most likely to compensate for the dysfunction of the existing unitary system. Truly, Iran's continuing civil strife is the result of a genuine and legitimate revolutionary mass movement. The Ayatollah Revolution has the potential for both increased "rising expectations" and "rising alienation." And if the existing situation continues, there is real danger that rising alienation could turn against the revolution itself. In light of its past experience, Iran has little choice but to move toward a federal system. A failure to do so could very well lead to the breakup of the country.

NOTES

1. George Ball, "Iran's Revolution Isn't Over Yet," *The Washington Star* (March 15, 1979), p. A-8.
2. See Bruce Maynard Borthwick, *Comparative Politics of the Middle East* (Englewood Cliffs, New Jersey: Prentice-Hall, Inc., 1980), pp. 185-219.
3. *U.S. News & World Report,* "The Rebellious Tribe in Russia's Path," (February 4, 1980), p. 22.
4. Robert G. Irani, *American Diplomacy: An Option Analysis of the Azerbaijan Crisis, 1945-1946* (Washington, D.C.: Institute of Middle Eastern and North African Affairs, Inc., 1978), pp. 21-22.
5. Enver M. Koury and Emile A. Nakhleh (ed.,), *The Arabian Peninsula, Red Sea, and Gulf: Strategic Considerations* (Washington, D.C.: Institute of Middle Eastern and North African Affairs, Inc., 1979), pp. 45-49.
6. See Carleton Coon, *Caravan* (New York: Henry Holt and Company, 1951), Chapter 1 and 10
7. *The Washington Post,* "Iranian Aid Predicts Kurds Will Escalate Guerrilla Campaign," (September 19, 1979), p. A-17.
8. *The Middle East Journal,* "Constitution of the Islamic Republic of Iran," Vol. 34, No. 2 (Spring 1980), pp. 184-204, and Article 19.
9. *Ibid.,* Article 12.
10. Jonathan C. Randal, "Kurds' Autonomy Cries Rekindle Ethnic Flashpoint in Iran," *The Washington Post* (March 2, 1979), p. A-13.
11. Jonathan C. Randal, "Iranian Troops Move to End Tabriz Battle," *The Washington Post* (December 10, 1979), p. A-20.
12. William Branigin, "Iran Confronts Separatism Among Tribal Minorities." *The Washington Post* (February 21, 1979), p. A-10.
13. Ted R. Gurr, *Why Men Rebel* (Princeton, New Jersey: Princeton University Press, 1970), p. 24.
14. James A. Bill, "Iran and the Crisis of '78," *Foreign Affairs* (Winter 1978/79), p. 332.
15. Robert Graham, *Iran: The Illusion of Power* (New York: St. Martin's Press, 1979), p. 216.
16. *Ibid.*
17. *Ibid.*
18. *Ibid.* pp. 215-16.
19. *Time,* "Through Blood and Fire," (December 24, 1979), p. 12.
20. Willian Branigin, "Cozying Up to Khomeini: Futile Policy," *The Washington Post* (September 23, 1979), p. C-3.
21. See David Sutcliffe, "Mob Law—in the Name of the Imam," *Arab Month,* Vol. 1, No. 12 (September 1979), p. 24.
22. Terry Povey, "Iran's Autonomy Seekers," *The Middle East,* No. 58 (August 1979), pp. 41-42.
23. R. K. Ramazani, "Iran's Revolution In Perspective," in *The Impact of the Iranian Events Upon Persian Gulf & United States Security* (Washington, D.C.: American Foreign Policy Institute, 1979), p. 32.
24. Terry Povey, "Iran's New Constitution," *The Middle East,* No. 64 (February 1980), p. 30.
25. *Ibid.*
26. Graham, *op. cit.*, p. 217.
27. Povey, "Iran's New Constitution," *op. cit.*, p. 31.
28. *Ibid.*
29. *Ibid.*
30. *Ibid.*
31. *The Middle East Journal,* "Constitution of the Islamic Republic of Iran," *op.cit.*, Articles 5 and 107.

32. *Ibid.*, p. 184.
33. *Ibid.*, Article 109.
34. Edward Cody, "Troops Sent to Quell Violence in Tabriz," *The Washington Post* (January 10, 1980), p. A-24.
35. David Sutcliffe, "Our Leader is Not Elected—He Emerges," *Arab Month,* Vol. 2, No. 2 (November 1979), p. 14.
36. *The Middle East Journal,* "Constitution of the Islamic Republic of Iran," *op. cit.,* Article 110.
37. *Ibid.,* Article 91.
38. *Ibid.,* Article 96
39. *Ibid.,* Article 57.
40. *Ibid.,* Article 110.
41. *Ibid.,* Article 162 and 158.
42. Irani, *op. cit.,* pp. 16-24.
43. Ramazani, *op. cit.,* p. 34.
44. For more information see J. David Singer (ed.), *Quantitative International Politics* (New York: Free Press, 1968), pp. 87-88.
45. *Ibid., pp. 123-158.*
46. See William Coplin and Charles Kegley (ed.,), *Multimethod Introduction to International Politics* (Chicago: Markham, 1971), p. 42.
47. Ramazani, *op. cit.,* p. 31.
48. *The Middle East journal,* "Constitution of the Islamic Republic of Iran," *op. cit.,* Preamble, p. 187.
49. *Ibid.,* Article 19, p. 191.
50. Stuart Auerback, "Iran Constitution Ratified but Minorities Shun Vote," *The Washington Post* (December 5, 1979), p. A-16.
51. Jonathan C. Randal, "Iran Seeks to Curb Separatist Feeling Among Baluchis," *The Washington Post* (March 12, 1979), p. A-14.
52. Cnris de Dretser, "Iran's Troops Fight Kurds; Unrest Grows," *The Washington Post* (August 24, 1979), p. A-15.
53. Jonathan C. Randal, "Iranian-Kurdish Confrontation Relaxes," *The Washington Post* (November 23, 1979,), p. A28.
54. Terry Povey, "Iran's Abol-Hassan Bani-Sadr," *The Middle East,* No. 66 (April 1980), pp. 11-12.
55. Ole R. Holsti, *Crisis Escalation War* (Montreal: McGill-Queen's University Press, 1972), p. 145.
56. Michael Weisskopf, "Regionalism Seen as New Phase in Iran's Revolution," *The Washington Post* (January 11, 1980), p. A-18.
57. *The Washington Post,* "Kurds Vow 'All-Out War' on Iran's Islamic Government," (August 26, 1979), p. A-23.
58. Weisskopf, "Regionalism Seen as New Phase in Iran's Revolution," *op. cit.,* p. A-18.
59. Sutcliffe, "Our Leader Is Not Elected—He Emerges," *op. cit.,* p.14.
60. Randal, "Iran Seeks to Curb Separatist Feeling Among Baluchis," *op. cit.,* p. A-14
61. Weisskopf, "Regionalism Seen as New Phase in Iran's Revolution," *op. cit.,* p. A-18.
62. *Time,* "Another Ayatollah Is Angry," (December 24, 1979), p. 15.
63. *Ibid.*
64. *Ibid.,* p. 16.
65. Randal, "Iran Seeks to Curb Separatist Feeling Among Baluchis," *op. cit.,* p. A-14

66. Jonathan C. Randal, "Azerbaijan: Camal's Tail is Twisted," *The Washington Post* (December 12, 1979), p. A-33.
67. Nicholas Cumming Bruce, "Attack on Iranian Mosque Sparks Anti-Arab Conflict," *The Washington Post* (July 16, 1979), p. A-12.
68. William Branigin, "Arabs Demonstrate in Iran, Demand Regional Autonomu," *The Washington Post* (April 28, 1979), p. A-19.
69. Jonathan C. Randal, "Iranian Province Split Over Khomeini," *The Washington Post* (December 8, 1979), p. A-12.

V. U.S. SECURITY IN THE PERSIAN GULF: AN ASSESSMENT

Lisa deFilippis

The United States' search for a security policy in the Persian Gulf region reflects a broader quest for an effective American foreign policy in the world as a whole. In the decades following World War II the United States has tried two basic strategies. First was the policy of containment, exemplified by the Truman Doctrine. The second was regional partnership, following the guidelines of the Nixon Doctrine.

Under the policy of containment the United States took upon itself the responsibility for maintaining regional stability and preventing Soviet encroachment. This policy necessitated the proliferation of U.S. military installations and military alliances throughout the world. In the Persian Gulf region the containment policy led to the creation of the Baghdad Pact and later, the CENTO Alliance, which was organized to assure the "Northern Tier" countries that their independence would be protected from Soviet expansionism.

The major shift in U.S. foreign policy from containment to regional partnership was largely a reaction to U.S. involvement in Vietnam and reflected America's desire to avoid entangling its own forces in local conflicts in other parts of the world. The policy, outlined by President Nixon on the island of Guam in 1969, called for partnership between the United States and regional powers. The U.S. would support these countries with military and other aid to enable them to act as protectors of regional stability. In the Persian Gulf, Iran and Saudi Arabia were the nations considered most able to assume the role of regional stabilizers. Iran, however, took on the greater share of the burden because of its greater military capability and the apparent convergence of Nixon's policy with the regional power aspirations of the Shah of Iran. The policy necessitated the sale of sophisticated arms on a large scale. The Shah, eager to modernize Iran's military, used his status as regional partner to pressure the U.S. into selling him even more weapons than many considered necessary. This policy dominated U.S. foreign relations in the Gulf throughout the 1970s, and as a result, Iran was seen as crucial to the safeguarding of American interests in the Gulf.

The fall of the Shah has necessitated a re-evaluation of U.S. policy. The debate on U.S. policy after the Iranian revolution focuses on two alternatives: the possibility of direct military involvement versus the possibility of a new regional partner to replace Iran. If Vietnam taught the U.S. the potential dangers of containment, the crisis in Iran seems to have taught the pitfalls of regional partnership. In the course of this study the relative advantages and disadvantages of the two broad strategies will be considered.

The Persian Gulf is vital to the United States for a number of reasons Strategically, the U.S. must be concerned with its proximity to the Soviet Union, and, therefore, the Gulf's vulnerability to Soviet pressure and potential infiltration. Economic interests are also at stake, especially the vital interest in oil. There are also political and diplomatic interests in the area, related to the Arab-Israeli conflict; the U.S. would like Arab friends in order to facilitate the peaceful resolution of the conflict.

In the past decade several events occurred which greatly increased U.S. stakes in the area. The British had maintained regional stability in the Gulf since early in the nineteenth century. Their withdrawal from "east of Suez" in 1971 left the United States with added responsibility in the region. The next major event which added to the importance of the Gulf was the 1973 Arab oil embargo. Oil prices quadrupled at a time when the Western world's consumption and need for imported oil was on the rise. The oil embargo proved a rude awakening for Americans; made aware for the first time of their dependence on foreign oil, and the vulnerability of such dependence. Furthermore, America was forced to recognize the power held by the oil-producing states, using their oil as a political weapon. The hike in oil prices exacerbated the arms sales problem; the United States sought to sell more arms to offset the damage to the balance of payments and to tap the swelling treasuries of the oil-producing countries. The result of the oil embargo and price rise was that oil became, as Emile Nakhleh put it, "a major determinant of policy in both the producing countries and the United States."[1] Finally the 1970s have seen what many Persian Gulf states consider to be an alarming advancement of Soviet influence in the area geographically surrounding the Gulf. Recent Soviet advances in Afghanistan, and earlier in Ethiopia, in addition to the pro-Soviet government in South Yemen represent what appear to be significant gains in the region.

The events of 1970s, then, have made the development of a new policy for securing United States' interests in the Persian Gulf even more critical. In 1973 at Hearings before the House Foreign Affairs Subcommittee on the Near East and South Asian Affairs, James Noyes, then Deputy Assistant of Defense for Near East, African, and South Asian Affairs, refined U.S. interests in the Gulf as follows:

> 1-Containment of Soviet military power within its present borders;
> 2-Access to Persian Gulf oil;
> 3-Continued free movement of United States ships and aircraft into and out of the area.[2]

At the same Hearings Joseph Sisco, then Assistant Secretary of State for Near Eastern and South Asian Affairs, outlined American objectives in the Gulf as:

> 1-Support for indigenous regional collective security efforts to provide stability and foster orderly development without outside interference.

2-The peaceful resolution of territorial and other disputes among the regional states and the opening up of better channels of communication among them.
3-Continued access to Gulf oil supplies at reasonable prices and in sufficient quantities to meed our growing needs and those of our European and Asian Friends and allies.
4-Enhancing of our financial and commercial interests.

American policymakers were defining these interests virtually the same way throughout the 1970s.

 The United States pursued these interests and objectives by offering support for collective security arrangements, by encouraging the federation of Trucial States, by encouraging the states of the region to settle their territorial disputes, and by offering assistance in development programs. Most importantly, the United States sold arms to the States they felt capable of providing security for the Gulf region—primarily Iran and Saudi Arabia. The United States developed what came to be known as the "two pillars" policy. While Saudi Arabia primarily provided leadership in the Gulf based on its financial powers, Iran became the military "pillar". As Iran took up the mantle of "policeman" of the Gulf, the United States embarked on an arms sales policy of staggering dimensions. From 1972 to 1975, U.S. arms sales to Iran jumped from $524 million to $2.6 billion.[4] The United States considered these arms transfers to be an essential part of its policy.

 The Shah was anxious to cooperate with U.S. policy toward his country, because his perception of Iranian interests coincided well with U.S. interests in the area. He defined Iran's interests as preventing Soviet encroachment and advancement, both in Iran and throughout the Gulf; developing sufficient military strength to defend Iran against external aggression—primarily from Iraq—and to project Iranian power and influence in the Gulf; assuring the safe, uninterrupted flow of oil and other trade; preventing the radicalization of the Gulf by helping moderates remain in power; industrializing and modernizing Iran to insure a source of income when the oil runs out. From the Shah's perspective, the United States could help achieve many of his goals, both foreign and domestic. He saw the U.S. as Iran's only real protector against the Soviet Union. Furthermore, the United States was a willing supplier of the advanced weapons and training that would make Iran into a regional power, and of the technology necessary for domestic development and industrial expansion.

 The United States, too, reaped many benefits from Iran's role. The Shah's growing Navy provided security for western oil tankers. The Shah also helped guard against the spread of radicalism in the Persian Gulf area, notably when he sent Iranian troops to Oman in the early 1970s to help the Sultan quell the Marxist Dhofari rebels. This action and the high visibility of the Iranian Navy in the Gulf, especially around the strategic Strait of Hormuz, led Iran to be considered "policeman" of the Gulf. The U.S. further utilized Iran as a listening post to the USSR. Iran, of course, provided the U.S. a sure supply of oil; the Shah did not participate in the oil embargo. The Shah supplied both oil and diplomatic support to another major U.S. ally—Israel. The partnership between Iran and the United States, thus seemed to be mutually beneficial.

 When the Shah wanted more armaments, the U.S. supported the Shah's move to become the regional power. The U.S. sold him the weapons he felt he needed. As the price of oil escalated, it made a great deal of economic sense to sell arms to help the U.S. balance of payments. By the end of the 1970s the United States had come to rely quite heavily on Iran to protect American interests. The extent of American reliance on the Shah is evident by the uncertainty that characterized American policy after his fall.

The Iranian crisis demonstrates, *inter alia,* some of the serious drawbacks of the policy of regional partnerships. Clearly, Iran is no longer going to play its former role in maintaining Gulf security. Indeed, Iran at present is pursuing policies which seem to encourage instability in the region and throughout the Islamic world.

To what extent should American policy encourage the growth of political institutions and participation in the states of the Persian Gulf. Must the citizens of the Gulf states have a greater voice in their own governments before the Gulf can be made secure? Early in the 1970s analysts warned that the Shah was courting disaster by ignoring these needs in his country. Indeed, some analysts held that the U.S. actually exacerbated the problem. Marvin Zonis, in **Hearings** before the House Subcommittee on the Near East and South Asia in 1973, said: "I am very concerned that American foreign policy is contributing to the suppression and the postponement of fundamental social changes in Iran. These are going to come, if not now then in some time in the not too distant future."[5] Perhaps the United States needed to witness a revolution in Iran to learn just how important the encouragement of political participation can be—not only in the Gulf, but in other Third World States as well. Emile Nakhleh expressed this in his book *Arab-American Relations in the Persian Gulf:*

> Regional security for the U.S. or for Gulf states can be meaningful and enduring only in the context of domestic political stability in each state. Any new partnership on the regional or international level must be preceded by a domestic partnership between the government and its people. Only then can the U.S. hope to promote its interests in the Persian Gulf.[6]

Keeping in mind that U.S. policy must include the goal of political participation, one can return to the question of America's policy options in the Persian Gulf and the two general strategies outlined at the onset of this paper: an active military presence in the area or a substitute regional partner. A third possibility would be a combination of these two basic approaches.

The crux of the problem is who shall safeguard the security of the Gulf states, and by what means. This is not an easy task, as the threats to security come from both internal and external sources. In addition to the danger of Soviet incursion, there are worries about terrorist groups— seizing oil fields, hijacking oil tankers, or mining the Straits of Hormuz. (It is not difficult to envision a scenario in which a group of Palestinians or other extremists would take such actions in the hope of gaining political advantages.) Another danger lies in the growing preponderance of military power in Iraq. Who would discourage Iraqi adventurism to regain territory that has long been in dispute with Iran or Kuwait? Finally there is always the potential for internal upheavals within the states themselves.

Saudi Arabia, already considered the "second pillar" of U.S. regional partnership, would seem an obvious choice as guarantor of Gulf security. The Saudis already provide political and diplomatic leadership to the smaller states of the Gulf. There are, however, limits to Saudi Arabia's military potential that cast doubts on its ability to assume a "policeman" role. Saudi Arabia is not heavily populated. Consequently its armed forces are rather small, its naval capability limited. In fact, it is not at all certain that the Kingdom's armed forces would be capable of defending its own territory, including the oil fields against attack. Saudi Arabia, therefore, should not be expected to take Iran's place in the Gulf.

Early in 1979 after the Shah's abdication, President Carter hinted that Egypt as a moderate Middle Eastern state with considerable military potential and with common security concerns in the Red Sea and the Gulf area might be the logical "second pillar" (with the Saudis moving into the "first pillar" position). The *New York Times* reported Carter as saying that Egypt could become a "legitimate stabilizing force in protecting the smaller nations in the region."[7] In fact, Sadat volunteered Egypt for the job. He reportedly told Defense Secretary Harold Brown that Egypt would help police the Middle East in return for heavy infusions of modern arms.[8] In the spring of 1979 Egypt was said to have sent troops to the Sultan of Oman to replace the Iranian troops that had been dispatched at the time of the Dhofari rebellion.[9] If these reports are accurate, they would give substance to the Egyptian desire to help maintain security in the region. There is, however, a problem with this role for Egypt; Egypt is diplomatically isolated from the rest of the Arab world as a result of the Camp David Treaty with Israel. (Oman and the Sudan are the only other Arab nations to support the treaty). No state in the Gulf, except Oman, appears inclined to accept Egyptian help.

In spite of these problems the United States has attempted to continue the regional partnership policy. In the past this has meant increased arms sales; in the fiscal year ending October 1979 the U.S. sold $5 billion in arms to Saudi Arabia, five times the amount sold to Israel in the same year.[10] Also the sale of 60 F-15's to Saudi Arabia was approved by Congress, with deliveries to start in 1981. This sale is accompanied by training and technical assistance "packages" and, therefore, represents a considerable U.S. commitment to Saudi Arabia. In late October the Pentagon announced plans to build major complexes to base and maintain these planes, a construction project worth $1.5 billion. The Pentagon argued in favor of the project: "Saudi Arabia remains the cornerstone for attaining U.S. foreign policy objectives in the Arabian Peninsula and adequate F-15 basing will improve the deterrent capabilities of the Royal Saudi Arabian Air Force."[11]

Another indication of U.S. commitment to the regional partnership policy was its response to Saudi Arabia's plea for over 300 million dollars worth of arms for North Yemen. The United States felt the sale was absolutely necessary to reassure the Saudis of continued American support in the Gulf. William F. Crawford, Acting Secretary for the Near East and South Asia, described the action as designed to "indicate the seriousness with which we view this situation and our determination to meet the defense needs of moderate governments in this strategically vital part of the world."[12]

This action generated a great deal of criticism. The decision had been made at the executive level—waiting Congressional review—by invoking the emergency clauses of the Arms Export and Control Act. More importantly, critics of the arms sale questioned the wisdom of exporting sophisticated weapons to governments, even friendly ones, in areas of great instability. This criticism points up one of the major problems with the regional partnership approach of U.S. foreign policy.

Throughout the 1970s the position of the U.S. government was that major arms sales were necessary to U.S. security in the Persian Gulf. Joseph Sisco explained this policy in 1975 at Hearings before a Special Subcommittee of the House Committee on International Relations:

> Our whole policy (in the Persian Gulf since the British left in 1971) has been based on the major premise that the two key countries in this area are Saudi Arabia and Iran and that to the degree which the U.S. could promote cooperation between these two . . . we would be contributing to stability in the region. We believe that arms policies that we have pursued, in particular have contributed not only to their greater regional cooperation, but to help meet what they consider and perceive to be their security concerns in the area.[13]

When the U.S. does not wish to commit its own military forces to the Gulf region, yet recognizes the importance of security in the area, the regional actors who are expected to be "pillars" of security, must be supplied with adequate military resources for the job.

Critics of the arms sales policy in the Gulf do not oppose arms sales *per se*, but argue against the seemingly uncontrolled nature of the sales, both in terms of quantity and level of sophistication. The primary objective seems to be a dangerous U.S. precedent of selling all the weapons requested. It was feared that arms transfers would lead to an arms race in the Gulf, as each nation sought to obtain the same weapons as its neighbor. Further, while the Administration claimed that the arms sales were necessary for stability in the region, others argued that they led to even greater instability and that armed conflict became more likely as the availability of weapons increased. The sales also necessitated greater American involvement in the countries of the Gulf for training and for the servicing of the weapons. The fear was expressed—and now it is known to be a realistic one—that the presence of so many Americans in the area might give rise to anti-Americanism.[14] The arms sales, too, placed a heavy burden on the social systems of the states of the Gulf. Arms purchases channel money away from development programs. In countries with large populations like Iran, this can and in fact seems to have led to popular dissatisfaction with the government. This dissatisfaction in turn leads to the very sort of instability that the policy was designed to prevent.

Arms transfers are but one of the serious disadvantages of the regional partnership approach. There are others which are clearly demonstrated by the Iranian Revolution and are frequently invoked by the press and the government as "lessons of Iran". Another of the pitfalls of the policy is U.S. reliance on the regime in power. If the regime is overthrown, America is identified with the unpopular government and consequently the U.S. position in the country is seriously damaged. The other side of the coin is the discrediting of the regime itself through too close an association with the United States. As Marvin Zonis told the House Subcommittee on the Near East and South Asia in 1973: "Unless the regime (in Iran) can dissociate itself more completely from our government (the U.S.), it will be troubled by widespread doubts as to its policies and loyalties."[15] A further danger is the uncertainty of large amounts of sophisticated weapons remaining in the nation to which they were sold. The weapons could always be transferred to other countries. They might in fact be used in some future conflict with Israel. There is also the danger that the country receiving the weaponry might be overtaken by an unfriendly regime. A hostile government would then have access to American weapons. A final problem with the regional partnership approach is that other countries do not always see American interests as their own and sometimes act in ways that are not ideal for the U.S.

If the United States cannot count on any other nation to protect its interests in the Gulf, then it must act to protect these interests itself. This would necessitate adopting an enhanced military presence in the area. In the past year there have been signs that the U.S. has been doing just that. One of the primary tasks for the U.S. has been to reassure Gulf states that America is committed to security in the area. Increasing the U.S. military presence was considered one of the ways to do this. Since no Gulf state would tolerate U.S. forces being stationed on their soil, most of the increased military presence takes the form of air force or naval visits on what are known as "flag-showing" missions. The Defense Department uses the Iranian example to press for expanded military presence in the Gulf and Indian Ocean. It suggests frequent appearances of naval vessels; the expansion of the naval base at Diego Garcia; and feasibility studies of United States military intervention into the area. In fact Defense Secretary Brown remarked several times since the fall of the Shah that the U.S. would use military force to protect its vital interests in the Gulf area.[16] It is not clear, however, whether the U.S. would be able to do so successfully. Some defense analysts point out that the United States lacks sufficient air transportation.[17]

The Iranian Revolution has sparked renewed interests in Secretary Brown's idea of a quick-strike force that would enable the United States to deploy troops rapidly to a crisis area in which no American troops were regularly stationed.[18] Although the United States would not maintain bases in the Gulf area *per se*, an enhanced military presence would suggest, as Secretary Brown put it, that the "less intrusive and less obvious forms of U.S. presence or possibility military influence, such as ship visits and so on, are clearly the right way to begin such activities."[19]

Another possibility for increased military involvement in the area is the expansion of U.S. naval forces, perhaps through the creation of a fleet for the Indian Ocean—the Fifth Fleet.[20] The United States has not had, until recently, a significant naval presence in the Indian Ocean and since 1977 has been engaged in talks with the Soviet Union in talks aimed at setting limits for naval deployments there. If the United States were to increase its Navy substantially in the Indian Ocean, it is possible, however, that the Soviet Union would expand rather than limit their already sizable naval force there.

The dangers of an increased American military presence in the Gulf include the possibility that a military intervention could escalate into war. This failure of deterrence might be compounded by the danger that U.S. economic interests in the area could not be secured by military force. The authors of a Congressional Research Service report to the Senate Foreign Relations Committee in 1979 wrote:

The real utility of military power to securing economic objectives has not been established given the ease with which oil fields and port facilities could be put out of action during any attempt by an external power to obtain resources through military means.[21]

The United States seems to be avoiding the choice of one strategy, either regional partnership or containment, to the total exclusion of the other. The Iranian Revolution generated a great deal of insecurity among the Gulf states which fear something similar happening in their own countries. They also fear that the United States might step aside as it has been criticized as doing in the case of the Shah. While U.S. policy in response to the Iranian Revolution has not been consistent, it appears that the United States has been trying to reassure allies and friends of its concern for the security of the Gulf and of its intent to act on this concern. Since the Iranian Revolution, U.S. F-15's have visited Saudi Arabia, naval forces have been deployed in the Gulf, and arms sales to friendly states in the area have increased (Saudi Arabia, Egypt, North Yemen, the Sudan, Oman, and Jordan). More recently, AWACS, early warning aircraft, have been sent to Saudi Arabia, and a joint exercise was held with Egypt.

Many Gulf states, however, appear to believe that the United States does not take the Soviet threat seriously enough. The Sultan of Oman, for example, thinks that the Soviet Union is maneuvering to acquire control of the Persian Gulf. "The objective is not to deny the Western world its oil, but to acquire strategic control through its proxies in the area."[22] Consequently, the Gulf states want the United States to increase its military commitment to the area. More specifically they want the United States to demonstrate its interest and support by supplying them with additional military hardware.

Though the dangers of large arms sales have received much attention following the fall of the Shah, it appears that the countries of the Gulf continue to see arms sales as the indication of American commitment. Bernard Weinraub, writing for the *New York Times*, quoted an American official as saying, "Believe me, we're not permitted by events to be as confident as we were in the early 1970s when arms sales were meant to be a pillar of strength."[23] Yet the U.S. falls back on the arms sales to demonstrate its interest and to reassure nervous allies. This dilemma has been expressed by another American official, who accompanied Secretary Brown on his February 1979 trip to the Middle East:

> We didn't come out here to sell arms, we came out to reassure these countries we are interested in stability of the region. Yet people fall back and just want to do business as usual. They ask for weapons. That's the real irony.[24]

The Gulf nations are primarily interested in providing for their own security needs. They want to rely on their own strength to protect their territory and independence against any perceived threats. It is not surprising that the nations of the Gulf seek to expand their military power, particularly in view of the increasing Gulf instability. The United States, however, is faced with the question of whether expanding arms sales are in the best interest of the United States or even in the best interest of the Gulf states. Unfortunately, there is no clear answer.

It seems advisable that the U.S. should seek a balanced policy in the

Gulf and encourage cooperative security schemes among the Gulf states, instead of relying on one country alone as the guarantor of security. The United States should foster friendships with many states in the area and should project a stronger military presence in the Gulf and in surrounding areas, while not becoming too closely associated with any regime in power. One way to accomplish this has been suggested by Professor Rouhollah K. Ramazani: the United States should "try and persuade other advanced industrial countries in OECD to join in common efforts to develop both economic and security ties with Gulf states. . ."[25] Professor Ramazani seeks to spread out American ties among a number of Gulf states, thus guarding against the backlash of anti-Americanism experienced in Iran.

On 23 January 1980 President Carter announced his commitment to the security of the Persian Gulf region. Addressing the Congress in his third State of the Union message, he warned that "any attempt by any outside force to gain control of the Persian Gulf region will be regarded as an assault on the vital interests of the United States. . . . Such an assault will be repelled by use of any means necessary including military force."[26] This policy, the "Carter Doctrine," has been heralded as a major turning point in American foreign policy. "For the first time since the high point of involvement in the Vietnam War a decade ago, the United States would be increasing its military force and security responsibilities in a faraway region rather than reducing them."[27]

This policy appears to represent a shift toward containment and away from regional partnership. While regional partnership is not being abandoned entirely (Arms transfers to Egypt, for example, are at their highest level ever.). Carter's strategy involves an increased military posture in the area. The Soviet action in Afghanistan has accelerated this trend toward a more pronounced military strategy, both in the Gulf and in the Indian Ocean.

Carter's actions supporting American policy in the Gulf include requests for appropriations for ship-building (naval deployments in the Indian Ocean) and for transport aircraft (rapid deployment). Finally, the Administration has sought agreements granting American access to military facilities in the region, notably Oman, Somalia, and Kenya. Access to such bases enhances the ability of the United States to project armed strength into the area without creating U.S.-owned bases that are so unpopular to Third World states. As Carter indicated. the U.S. must maintain a lower profile. It cannot protect the Gulf without the aid of allies and local states. Thus American policy, even while tilting toward containment, must continue to rely on regional partnerships if it is to be successful in securing "vital" American interests in the Persian Gulf.

Ultimately, the United States must reduce its dependence on the oil that so complicates American policy in the Persian Gulf, and must help the states of the area develop sound internal political systems. The U.S. position would also be greatly improved by a settlement of the Palestinian problem. This issue, and the U.S. stance on it, continue to inpede fully cooperative relations with all Arab states. Until these goals are accomplished, security for American interests in the Gulf will prove elusive.

NOTES

1. *Arab-American Relations in the Persian Gulf,* (Washington, D.C.: American Enterprise Institute for Public Policy Research, 1975), p. 62.
2. U.S. Congress, House, Committee on Foreign Affairs, *New Perspectives on the Persian Gulf,* Hearings before the Subcommittee on the Near East and South Asia of the Committee on Foreign Affairs. 93rd Cong., 1st Sess., 1973, p. 39.
3. *Ibid.,* p. 2
4. U.S. Congress, House, Committee on International Relations, *The Persian Gulf, 1975: The Continuing Debate on Arms Sales,* Hearings before the Special Subcommittee on Investigations of the Committee on International Relations. 94th Cong., 1st Sess., 1976, p. v.
5. *New Perspectives on the Persian Gulf,* p. 65.
6. Nakhleh, p. 53.
7. *New York Times,* February 23, 1979.
8. *New York Times,* March 8, 1979.
9. David Lynn Price, "Moscow and the Persian Gulf," *Problems of Communism,* March-April 1979, pp. 1-13
10. *Washington Post,* October 11, 1979.
11. *Washington Post,* October 25, 1979.
12. *Department of State Bulletin,* June 1979, p. 40.
13. *The Persian Gulf, 1975,* p. 6.
14. Edward M. Kennedy, "The Persian Gulf: Arms Race or Arms Control," *Foreign Affairs* 54 (October 1975): 14-35.
15. *New Perspectives on the Persian Gulf,* p. 70.
16. *New York Times,* February 26, 1979.
17. *Washington Post,* October 3, 1979.
18. *New York Times,* April 20, 1979.
19. *New York Times,* February 26, 1979.
20. Juan Cameron, "Our What-if Strategy for Mideast Trouble Spots," *Fortune,* May 7, 1979, pp. 155-160.
21. U.S. Congress, Senate, *United States Foreign Policy Objectives and Overseas Military Installations.* Prepared for the Committee on Foreign Relations by the Foreign Affairs and National Defense Division, Congressional Research Service, Library of Congress. Committee Print. Washington, D.C.: U.S. Government Printing Office, 1979, p. 121.
22. Arnaud de Bourchgrave, "Oman: in Dire Straits," *Newsweek,* September 24, 1979, p. 61.
23. *New York Times,* February 18, 1979.
24. *Ibid.*
25. Rouhollah K. Ramazani, "Security in the Persian Gulf," *Foriegn Affairs* 57 (Spring 1979): p. 833.
26. *New York Times,* January 27, 1980.
27. *Washington Post,* January 24, 1980.

VI. REACTIONS TO IRAN'S REVOLUTION: THE SEARCH FOR SECURITY

Charles G. MacDonald

The Iranian Revolution has signaled the coming of a new revolutionary era in which Third World governments face new forces of change. These forces, fueled in part by religious zeal and also by a resurgent nationalism, seek to redress past inequities and to reestablish a Third World self-esteem that has been lost in fruitless efforts of "catch up" with the West. In Iran's case the rising expectations that accompanied the increasing oil revenues and the royal proclamations anticipating the "era of the Great Civilization," were only to be frustrated by economic bottlenecks, corruption in high places, and perhaps worst of all, inflation. The Shah's government, despite its White Revolution, promises of reform, friendship with the United States, and sophisticated military arsenals, lost its legitimacy in the eyes of the Iranian people. The last-ditch liberalization efforts of the Shah, who legalized political parties, freed many political prisoners, and allowed for the return of political exiles, did little to rally support around the monarchy and perhaps hastened its demise. The opponents of the Shah were able to build upon a legacy of political repression, an omnipresent fear of SAVAK, and the growing economic failures to force the Shah from power and end the monarchy.

The Islamic Republic of Iran that emerged under the guidance of Ayatollah Khomeini was built upon Islamic principles on the one hand and anti-imperialistic rhetoric on the other. The advocacy of the export of its Islamic Revolution to other governments in the Gulf and throughout the Middle East has become a major concern for the target states. This new Islamic militancy now rivals communism and Arab socialism as the vehicle for revolutionary change in the contemporary Middle East.

In addition to spawning new revolutionary pressures, the Iranian Revolution has created a new "vacuum of power" in the Gulf. The removal of the Shah effectively ended Iran's "policeman role" and left the Gulf without a stabilizing power. The Soviet invasion of Afghanistan, the seizure of the American hostages, and the Iran-Iraq war have each raised new security concerns throughout the Middle East and have heightened those in the Gulf. The aftermath of the Iranian Revolution has led Middle Eastern governments to reevaluate their policies in an effort to bolster their domestic legitimacy and strengthen their respective defenses. The purpose of this chapter is to explore some of the policy responses of three key states--Saudi Arabia, Iraq, and Egypt. The policy trends that relate to security are emphasized.

SECURITY INTERESTS IN PERSPECTIVE

Generally speaking, the security interests of Saudi Arabia, Iraq, and Egypt throughout the postwar period have been vulnerable to the vicissitudes of inter-Arab politics. At times the three states have been allies; at times they have been opponents. Their relations with the superpowers have also fluctuated. While Saudi Arabia has traditionally been hostile to Soviet overtures in the area, its relations with the United States have varied. Saudi Arabia did not join the Baghdad Pact or CENTO, but has consistently looked to the United States for military assistance. Iraq was at first in the Western camp and was a member of the Baghdad Pact, but then moved after 1958 into the Soviet sphere and became a Soviet client state. More recently, Iraq has not only exhibited definite signs of nonalignment, but has made overtures to the West, especially to Europe. Egypt's superpower relationships have also changed. After Nasser's pioneering effort at nonalignment in the 1950s, Egypt moved into the Soviet sphere. An abrupt change in Egypt's direction was made by Sadat, who has turned Egypt to the West.

Despite the changing security relationships of Saudi Arabia, Iraq, and Egypt, relative to each other in inter-Arab circles and with respect to the superpowers, the states have shared a certain commonality of interest in the broader and abstract concept of "Arab security." In terms of the Arab-Israeli conflict, they have shared the search for a solution to the Palestinian question, even though their policies on tactics and final goals have not always coincided. Egypt's peace initiatives through the Camp David Accords and the Egyptian-Israeli Treaty were strongly opposed by Saudi Arabia and Iraq. Egypt's recent arms assistance to Iraq during the Iran-Iraq war could signal a new opening for the renewal of relations between Egypt and the Gulf states. Although their economies and the welfare of their populations vary, Egypt, Iraq, and Saudi Arabia share a common interest in maintaining internal stability against revolutionary pressures. Iran and Libya have openly challenged the legitimacy of their respective governments.

SAUDI ARABIA

In the aftermath of the Iranian Revolution Saudi security priorities have emphasized an immediate concern with internal stability and a long-run desire to build a defensive capability. Saudi policy, while reflecting an appreciation of the Shah's difficulties, has maintained a positive orientation of building preparedness, rather than being overly reactive. Like the Shah's Iran, Saudi Arabia has a monarchical regime, has been closely associated with the United States, and has been experiencing rapid modernization. Saudi Arabia has also come to face inflation, corruption, and even budget deficits, but not the economic disappointments that were so visible in Iran. Accordingly, Saudi security policy has not focused upon economics, but has sought to strengthen its external and internal defenses, including a conscious effort to promote the government's legitimacy.

External Defense

Saudi policy aimed at defending against an overt attack has two basic dimensions. First, Saudi Arabia must consider the possibility of an overt attack from a superpower, but has no military capability to thwart such an attack. In this regard, Saudi Arabia is particularly suspicious of Soviet intentions, especially with the Soviet presence in nearby Ethiopia and South Yemen and the growth of the Soviet naval capability in the Indian Ocean. Saudi Arabia, strongly critical of the Soviet actions in Afghanistan, can only look to the United States to deter overt Soviet aggression or any Soviet attempt to close the Strait of Hormuz. At the same time, Saudi Arabia is not unaware of its political differences with the United States over Israel and the Palestinians, and over the price and supply of oil. Thus, Saudi Arabia is not receptive to the stationing of an American Rapid Deployment Force on Saudi territory for fear that it could become a Trojan Horse.

Second, apart from a superpower threat, Saudi Arabia must consider an attack emanating from another state in the region, either against Saudi territory or that of a strategic neighbor. In 1979 after the Shah left Iran, Saudi Arabia looked to the United States for massive arms shipments to North Yemen when North Yemen was apparently attacked by South Yemen. The Saudi funding of these arms transfers indicated the seriousness that the Saudis attached to developments on their southern border. In October 1980 Saudi Arabia, fearing that Iran might expand the Iran-Iraq War by striking at Saudi oil fields, welcomed the arrival of four American AWACS. Although Saudi Arabia relies on the United States to deter a Soviet attack and looks to the United States for protection and assistance in emergency situations, Saudi Arabia has adopted the policy of acquiring a defensive capability, at least in the regional context, that would not rely on the assistance or approval of the United States. This position was emphasized at the Islamic Conference in Taif when Crown Prince Fahd warned that the security of the Islamic nation couldn't be assured by taking refuge under the umbrella of a superpower. The policy to strengthen Saudi defenses is reflected in Saudi Arabia's acquisition of sophisticated weaponry, not only from the United States, but also from other sources, such as France, Britain, and West Germany. Recent controversial requests of additional equipment for American F-15s, 5 American AWACS, and some 300 West German advanced Leopard II tanks and armored personnel carriers further suggest that Saudi Arabia wishes to build a defensive capability strong enough to meet any regional threat.

The Saudi decision to acquire a massive and sophisticated conventional arsenal resembles the often criticized, but similar, decision of the Shah, who also saw the need to "be able to go it alone." The Saudi desire to acquire the AWACS and other sophisticated weapons systems does not necessarily reflect an inherent distrust of the West, but rather an understanding of the political realities of the region that might prevent the United States from coming to Saudi Arabia's assistance. Saudi Arabia does not discount the possibility of an Israeli attack.

Internal Stability

Saudi Arabia is in the process of building a long-term defensive capability, but in the last two years it has focused greater attention upon internal stability. The Saudis are very much aware that the Shah fell from power because of internal developments, rather than from an external attack. Thus, Saudi Arabia depends only partially on its internal military strength; it has placed its primary emphases on promoting the legitimacy of the Saudi government and bolstering its internal security through bilateral security agreements and through the newly-formed Gulf Cooperation Council [GCC].

Saudi Arabia's government faced its first significant internal challenge when the Grand Mosque in Mecca was seized in November 1979. The attack on the Grand Mosque was led by a group of Islamic fanatics who claimed to support a *Mahdi* or Shiite Messiah, and the attack was reportedly linked to a disturbance in Medina. Later in November, riots were reported in Shiite areas near the Ras Tanura oil fields, especially at Qatif. The Shiite rioting, apparently not directly related to the seizure of the Grand Mosque, followed an earlier Shiite disturbance at the Grand Mosque when Hojatoleslam Ghaffari was to speak. Reports indicated that the Shiite rioters called for Saudi Arabia to support Iran's Islamic Revolution and to stop selling oil to the United States.

Although the Saudi security forces were able to handle the seizure of the Grand Mosque and the subsequent Shiite rioting, the incidents did indicate that the pressures of modernization were taking a toll. The ideas generated by the Islamic Revolution in Iran were becoming a dangerous threat to the Saudi royal family. The political overtones that accompanied the fanatics' charges of corruption in the royal family; their questioning of the Saudi's modernization efforts; and the calls for an end to television, professional soccer, and employment of women signaled an ominous mixing of the political and the religious.

In response to the challenge, the Saudi government moved to reaffirm its authority and to solidify its legitimacy in the eyes of the Saudi people. It sought to allay any fears that traditional Islamic values were being lost in a rush toward modernization. First, with a view to the Iranian experience, Saudi Arabia had clamped strict government censorship on all news of the Grand Mosque seizure, and later censored news of the Shiite disturbances. This was to avoid any "media-inspired" disturbances that had been so prevalent in Iran. Next, in a stern public display of its authority, Saudi Arabia beheaded 63 of those involved in the seizure of the Grand Mosque. The executions, held in January 1980, took place in Riyadh, Medina, and several other cities. Saudi Arabia emphasized its strict adherence to Islamic Law by additional actions, such as limiting the employment and travel of women, banning women's photographs in the press, and rigorously enforcing the rules relating to the five daily prayers. It might be noted that many such reforms actually predated the Mosque seizure.

Saudi Arabia also moved to solidify its legitimacy in several other ways. Being aware that the lack of political development in Iran was widely believed to be a major factor in the delegitimazation of the Shah, the Saudi government appeared to be moving in the direction of providing some form of limited political participation. Crown Prince Fahd announced 18 March 1980 the formation of a committee, chaired by Interior Minister Prince Naif, to draft plans for "a basic system of (Islamic) government" and a Shoura or "consultative council" (also termed a Peoples' Assembly or Senate). Such Saudi efforts to promote a genuine political participation moved forward slowly. Although such efforts were highlighted in the Saudi press in spring 1980, they reflected a much earlier decision of King Faisal. Saudi officials watched the results of the 1981 Kuwaiti elections very closely, especially the successes of the Islamic fundamentalists. Reacting to charges of corruption in the royal family concerning "commissions paid on business deals to royal princes" and the smuggling and drinking of alcohol,[1] Saudi officials emphasized that measures would be taken against "all those who harm the reputation of their country," including "members of the royal family in the first instance."[2] Thus, steps were apparently taken to limit the "high living" and in some cases, irresponsibility of members of the royal family.

To prevent possible charges of being a servant of American interests, especially with the receptiveness in the Gulf to the anti-imperialist and anti-American rhetoric broadcast from Iran, Saudi Arabia has pursued a policy that tends to keep the American government at a distance. Saudi Arabia has adamantly opposed the stationing of American forces in Saudi Arabia or in other Gulf states, and has repeatedly called for Gulf security to be provided by the Gulf states themselves. Prince Saud, the Saudi foreign minister, focused upon "Gulf security and defense" at the Taif Conference in 1979, and again asserted that "the task lies exclusively with the Gulf countries."[3] Major differences between Saudi policy and American policy are more readily apparent when Israel and the Palestinians are considered. Saudi Arabia has assumed a greater leadership role in the Islamic World. For example, Saudi Arabia openly called for a *jihad* of all Islamic states in response to Israel's move to annex East Jerusalem in August 1980. The Saudi call for a *jihad* did not seek to bring about a total holy war, but, as explained by Prince Saud, was a call for Arab and other Islamic states to combine their resources to safeguard holy rights. The call for a *jihad* against Israel that reappeared at the Third Islamic Conference at Taif in January 1981 similarly stressed "the moral and material aspects of *jihad*."

Saudi Arabia, apart from its efforts to promote the legitimacy of its government, adopted a policy of strengthening its internal security system through a series of bilateral agreements for security cooperation, and through the nascent Gulf Cooperation Council. While the Saudi government worked to remain in good favor with the Saudi populace, it also wanted to limit the subversive activities of Islamic militants, leftists, and foreign agents. The pan-Islamic activities of the Iranian revolutionaries and their ties to Syria, Libya, and various Palestinian groups had to be viewed as an immediate threat. Accordingly Saudi Arabia concluded a number of bilateral security agreements: with Iraq in February 1979; with South Korea in July 1979; with Tunisia in April 1980; and with Taiwan in April 1980, among others. An agreement with Bonn, signed in September 1980, reportedly provided for West Germany's special security force, the CSG-9, to train members of a "security crisis elite" of the Saudi SSF.[4] Moreover, negotiations for Pakistani security assistance, including the possible stationing of Pakistani forces in Saudi Arabia, were reported in their final states in December 1980.

In a departure from traditional Saudi policy of avoiding alliance, Saudi Arabia formally joined with Kuwait, Bahrain, Qatar, Oman, and the United Arab Emirates in February 1981 to form the "Cooperation Council for the Arab States of the Gulf," better known as the Gulf Cooperation Council (GCC). This represented a policy shift because King Khalid had said in May 1975 that ". . . cooperation in all fields among the gulf countries can be achieved even without the existence of such alliance."[5] The newly-formed GCC has stressed "co-ordination in all spheres, especially the economic and social ones." and appears to be an attempt to emulate the ten-member European Economic Community. While the GCC outwardly represents an effort to establish an integrated Arab community in the Gulf, implicit in the organization's formation is the desire to cooperate on internal security matters. Previous joint efforts, such as cooperation on passport control and immigration, are likely to be included under the GCC's authority.

The GCC and the various Saudi bilateral security agreements seem to be based upon and in accord with several basic principles set forth in a Saudi-sponsored security plan that was reportedly circulated at the end of 1980.[6] According to the plan, Saudi Arabia maintains that collective security could be achieved only if each Arab state were able to enjoy security and stability at home and if Arab states would respond to the requests of the states threatened by helping to combat local and imported sabotage, and by cooperating at the international level to deny international criminals and saboteurs access or refuge.[7] Saudi Arabia also asserts that the strengthening of cooperation among police forces of the various states, including instant communications and the exchange of information on criminals, is essential.[8] In this regard, Saudi Arabia's General Intelligence Department (GID) has already installed a "computer-assisted surveillance system" with branches at "airports, frontier posts, and major industrial complexes" and with a capability that could extend to other Gulf states by adding additional radio-linked computer terminals.[9]

In summary, Saudi policy trends indicate that serious attention has been focused upon internal stability, both in terms of promoting governmental legitimacy based upon Islam and in building a comprehensive internal security system that could be extended to neighboring states, possibly under the aegis of the GCC. Saudi Arabia also appears to be in the process of building a defensive capability that could deter aggressive acts by any regional power, without a reliance on a superpower.

IRAQ

The Iraqi reaction to the Iranian revolution has been much more dramatic than that of Saudi Arabia. Iraq, an Arab Baath Socialist Republic, is rent with religious, ethnic, and ideological dissension and appears more susceptible to Iranian efforts to export revolution. Thus, Iraq has responded not only with a concerted effort to build a sense of Iraqi nationalism and to remove any incentive to rebel against the central government of Saddam Hussein, but also by exercising its military option against revolutionary Iran.

Internal Stability

President Saddam Hussein's regime is one of contrasts. On the one hand it has appeared enlightened by encouraging education, political participation, and an economic development that includes a concern for welfare. On the other hand it has appeared medieval in its reaction to dissent and has not hesitated to use force internally and externally. It has provided handsome incentives to support the regime, but has dealt with opposition ruthlessly by Western standards.

Among the efforts to promote the legitimacy of the central government and a sense of national attachment, is the Iraqi government's emphasis on education. While opposition to the Shah was growing in 1978, Iraq was launching a forced education program that not only served to fight illiteracy, but also acted as a socializing program. It sought to teach the masses to appreciate their history, their Arab Baathist leadership, and the nature of the "Zionist" role in Palestine. Law #92 of 22 May 1978, establishing a "national comprehensive compulsory literacy campaign," created a legal obligation for illiterates between 15 and 45 years of age to attend school. Bringing to mind the Literacy Corps of the Shah, Iraq formed a corps of volunteer teachers known as the "Pioneers." Iraq provided fines and imprisonment for those who chose not to attend school. Iraq's efforts earned it UNESCO's 1979 prize for "the most effective literacy campaign in the world."[10]

Showing an effort to promote political participation, Iraq held elections in June 1980 and set up its first parliament since 1958. The election drew some 840 candidates for the 250 seats in the new National Assembly. Candidates were limited to those who believed in the principles of the progressive and socialist revolution of 1968 and included some women. Women were also permitted to vote. The Baathist won a comfortable victory, thus adding to Saddam Hussein's domestic legitimacy.

President Hussein has also sought to improve his regime's popularity in other ways. Iraq, like Saudi Arabia, is an oil power with proven oil reserves that promise many years of economic prosperity. Hussein has not hesitated to spend oil revenues to bolster support for his government, as indicated by his raising the salaries of the armed forces in July 1979. Iraq not only provided "free education," but also medical care and some subsidies for food and housing. As Iraq moves toward the goal of economic self-sufficiency, the various development projects, the acquisition of nuclear technology, and even the purchase of highly-sophisticated weapon systems are made possible by oil revenues. Such projects and acquisitions further contribute to the prestige of the Baathist regime.

Recognizing the importance of public relations, especially in the media, President Saddam Hussein has assumed a high visibility. He often appears on nightly television, being shown in constant contact with the Iraqi people. He is shown visiting villages and is often seen with children. The popular image thus created is made possible only with the presence of televisions. President Hussein also appears to be assuming leadership roles, both regionally and globally. In the Arab world Hussein espoused a new "Pan-Arab Charter" 8 February 1980.[11] The Pan-Arab Charter is comprised of eight principles that generally promote nonalignment vis-a-vis the superpowers, Arab solidarity against aggression, and the peaceful resolution of inter-Arab disputes. On a global level Hussein maintains a strong anti-imperialist stance and is quite active in the Nonaligned Movement. In fact, he is scheduled to follow Castro as President of the Nonaligned Movement.

President Saddam Hussein, despite his various positive efforts to broaden support for his government, has continued to face opposition from various groups. Among the major groups that have undertaken anti-government activities are communists, Kurdish dissidents, and Shiite extermists, including Iranian expatriates. Hussein's response to such opposition has been severe.

In 1978 the Iraqi Communist Party was purged from the government when it was discovered organizing cells in the Iraqi army. The purge saw a number of communist leaders summarily executed, and the party was forced to go underground. Again in 1979, shortly after Hussein became President, the Iraqi press reported widespread arrests, including 5 members of the Revolutionary Command Council, and 21 were reported executed by firing squads. In April 1980, as part of continuing government pressure on communists and other leftists, the offices of the Popular Front for the Liberation of Palestine and the Democratic Front for the Liberation of Palestine were ordered closed. To control dissent, the government has also banned many foreign magazines and newspapers, including some from the United States and Europe.

After the war with the Kurds ended in 1975, Iraq adopted a "carrot and stick" policy towards the Kurds. Unlike the Shah who limited national symbols among Iran's minorities, the Iraqi government granted significant autonomy to the Kurdish people, even permitting them to use the Kurdish language and maintain their own schools. The Kurds also received many material benefits from the oil revenues, including such consumer goods as televisions. Iraq's Vice President, Taha Mohieddin Maarouf, is a Kurd.

Iraq's policy towards the Kurds has been generally successful, but the Iranian revolution has raised new uncertainties. The fighting in Kurdish areas in Iran has threatened to spill over into Iraq. Iraq has worked with Turkey to keep the Kurdish situation under control. Currently two Kurdish groups, the Kurdistan National Union and the Unified Kurdistan Socialist Party, are included in the National Pan-Arab Democratic Front that is actively seeking to overthrow Saddam Hussein.

Posing the greatest potential threat to the Baathist regime are the Shiite Moslems in Iraq. Khomeini's expulsion from his Iraqi exile in 1978 created considerable resentment in the Shiite community. Iran's subsequent professed intention to export its revolution made neighboring Iraq a prime target, especially with its Shiite majority.

Iraq's internal response to Iranian efforts to foment revolution has been firm. In February 1980 Iraq established new restrictions on foreigners living in Iraq; those residents of more than five years that had not become Iraqi citizens were given 10-15 days to leave. In April 1980 when tensions flared, and Khomeini called upon Iraqis to rise up against Hussein's "imposed, inhuman, and illegal regime," Iraq expelled thousands of Iranians. Other severe measures have also been reported, including the execution of Shiite leader Ayatollah Bak'r Sad'r in Baghdad.

President Hussein's efforts to promote internal stability have certainly varied. Some have been positive; others have been repressive and open to criticism. Even more controversial, however, has been his use of force against the Islamic Republic of Iran.

Military Option

Before resorting to the use of force in September 1980, Iraq set the stage with public protestations and inter-Arab diplomacy. In October 1979 Iraq called upon Iran to agree "voluntarily" to reverse its 1975 accord with Iraq and return the entire Shatt al-Arab River to Iraqi control. Iraq also asserted that Iran should withdraw from Abu Musa and the Tunb

Islands, and should grant autonomy to its Arab, Kurdish, and Balouchi minorities. Iran did not respond favorably. In April 1980 Iranian-supported terrorists operations aimed at Iraqi officials and the reaffirmation of Iran's claim to Abu Musa and the Tunb Islands resulted in mutual accusations of subversion, repeated border incidents, the ouster of diplomats, and the placing of armies on alert.

Shortly after tensions receded, Iraq launched a diplomatic initiative to improve relations with certain Arab states. In May 1980 an agreement was reached with Jordan on economic and technical cooperation, apparently laying the groundwork for military cooperation. The agreement included Iraqi assistance in the development of Jordan's port of Aqaba and the improvement of Jordanian roads. The use of Aqaba as an alternative Iraqi port was apparently considered well in advance of the Iran-Iraq War. Iraq also worked to improve its ties with Kuwait, Saudi Arabia, and other Gulf states. In addition, Iraq continued its military buildup with purchases of highly-sophisticated weapons from both the Soviet Union and the West, especially France.

Following border incidents in early September 1980, Iraq charged 17 September that Iran had failed to return parts of Iraqi territory as provided in their 1975 agreement. Saddam Hussein declared the 1975 agreement "null and void" and renewed Iraq's claim to the entire Shatt al-Arab River. Iraqi air striked deep into Iran followed on 22 September and signaled the start of the Iran-Iraq War.

Iraq's motivations in resorting to a military option against revolutionary Iran remain open to debate and will probably be a subject of controversy for years to come. The initiation of the conflict was publicly tied to the failure of Iran to implement the 1975 treaty, but was undoubtedly the result of a complex set of factors that included Iranian efforts to subvert the Hussein regime, the weakening of the Iranian military, and the growing friendship between Iran and Syria. It might be argued that Iraq moved into Iran in self-defense in response to Iranian efforts to promote terrorism and foment revolution in Iraq. It could also be argued that Iraq acted aggressively to take advantage of Iran's uncertain internal situation in order to seize oil-rich Khuzistan, the Arab-populated Iranian province longsought by Iraq. In final analysis, it would be difficult to identify the single determining factor in Iraq's recourse to force against Iran since both defensive and offensive incentives were present. Iraq's military action, however, did establish a dangerous precedent in making population centers and oil facilities the targets of attack. The price to be paid by Iraq for its efforts to use force to stop the spread of the Iranian revolution, or for its own national aggrandizement, remains to be determined.

EGYPT

Egypt initially reacted strongly to the Iranian Revolution. President Sadat not only welcomed the Shah and granted him asylum, but openly called Ayatollah Khomeini a "lunatic" and charged that Khomeini misrepresented Islam. Sadat also scored other Moslem leaders for not speaking out against the Iranian excesses supposedly undertaken in the name of Islam. Sadat's hardline stance against Iran's revolution appeared to lessen somewhat when Egypt formally recognized Iran's Islamic government 1 November 1980. In early 1981 Egypt's sale of weapons to Iraq placed Egypt again in opposition to Iran while raising the possibility that Egypt's relations with the Arab Gulf states might improve.

Egypt has not been directly threatened by Iran, as Gulf states have, but has been strongly criticized in the Iranian media. Sadat has been condemned for his support of the Shah, his treaty with Israel, and his relationship with the United States.

Though not directly threatened by Iran, Egypt in especially sensitive to the revolutionary energies engendered by Ayatollah Khomeini's success. Sadat is quite aware that Egypt's poverty and economic problems make it susceptible to revolutionary rhetoric aimed at the masses, be it Islamic or communist. Egypt's problems are complex, but Sadat has maintained the initiative against revolutionary pressures just as he has internationally in his search for peace with Israel and the recognition of the legitimate rights of the Palestinian people.

Internal Stability

With Egypts's future stability by no means assured, Sadat has taken a number of internal measures to strengthen his government's legitimacy and to increase its authority to deal with dissent. He has sought to reform the political system, stress the significance of Islam within the state, and stabilize the economy, while improving the government's ability to deal with internal enemies.

Sadat took major steps toward political reform in 1979. To promote increased political participation and bring younger people into the political process, Sadat dissolved parliament and called for new elections following the signing of the peace treaty with Israel. The new elections, held in June 1979, were the first multi-party elections since 1952. One of Sadat's goals in calling for the new elections was the decentralization of the political system. Sadat wanted to place more responsibility with locally-electedofficials so that people could identify more closely with the government. In Iran the Shah had been so closely identified with the government that he was held personally responsible for the government's failures. In May 1980 Sadat announced further steps to decentralize the government by placing domestic policy under the control of provincial governors.

In other developments, the May 1980 referendum formally abolished the Arab Socialist Union, Nasser's "single party," and declared the new multi-party system official. In September 1980 elections were held for a new Consultative Council that is to advise the government. The National Democratic Party won all 140 seats contested, with the remaining 70 seats to be filled by Sadat's appointees.

In addition to promoting political participation Sadat also moved to place a new emphasis on the role of Islam in Egypt. Egyptian voters approved major changes in the 1971 Constitution in the referendum of 22 May 1980. The Sharia, the Islamic Code, was recognized as *the* principal source of law in Egypt, rather than *a* principal source. Egypt also paid increased attention to Islam in a number of other ways, from granting a special importance to Ramadan to publicly supporting Islamic Youth groups.[12]

Perhaps the most dangerous threat to the Sadat regime emanates from Egypt's troubled economic system. Accordingly, Sadat has focused his paramount attention on the faltering economy. In May 1980 he personally took full control of Egypt's internal affairs by assuming the additional post of premier in the hope of being able to improve Egypt's economic situation. On 14 May 1980 he identified new government actions to help the masses cope with inflation: the prices of 77 basic food and consumer products were reduced; the minimum wage was increased by 25%; social insurance was extended to cover virtually everyone; and the supplementary defense taxes were abolished. Later in 1980 Sadat stressed that the success of Egypt's government was dependent upon its ability to limit prices and provide food, and on 1 September he declared a one-month ban on the sale of local meat in order to curb the soaring meat prices. Sadat had asserted that progress could only come if there were peace with Israel. Now that a treaty has been signed, it is incumbent upon the Sadat regime to ensure that progress is forthcoming. If the rising expectations of the Egyptian people are frustrated, as those of the Iranian people were, revolution could easily follow.

In his 1981 May Day speech on the economy Sadat announced new increases in salaries and in subsidies on essential goods. He also pledged to keep prices fixed.[13] With the inflation rate about 30-35% and the government deficit increasing despite new oil revenues,[14] the Egyptian economy will not be easily stabilized. Moreover, Egypt must now import more than 35% of its food.[15] Whether President Sadat will be able to shore up the economy and shield Egypt from the revolutionary pressures that are sweeping the Middle East and Africa remains to be seen.

President Sadat's political liberalization, Islamic reform, and search for economic stability are ongoing, but so are the radical forces of change in Egypt. Sadat has responded with tough measures to deal with dissent. In March 1979 arrests of militant Islamic students were reported following incidents in Asyut. Some 60 members of the Egyptian Communist Party were reported in August 1979. To counter internal dissent and to strengthen the government's hand domestically, a new "anti-dissent" law was drawn up in January 1980. This was primarily aimed at controlling Egyptians, especially leftists, that were critical of the government and the political system. The law targeted supporters of doctrines opposed to "divine teachings"; those who expressed "contempt for Egypt's political, social or economic system"; those who advocated the "repudiation of popular religious, moral or national values"; and broadcasters or publishers of "false or misleading news or information that could inflame public opinion, generate envy and hatred, or threaten national unity or social peace."[16]

In March 1980 religious clashes in Asyut took several lives. The Coptic Church charged that Copts were being persecuted by Islamic militants. In April 1980 thousands of Moslem students demonstrated in Asyut to protest the presence of the Shah in Egypt and also the placement of Copts in the Sadat government. The government responded that it would not allow "extremist Moslems or Copts to stir up trouble." Egypt apparently will not tolerate domestic unrest, regardless of the source.

Gulf Security Role?

Egypt's security interests are complex, but primarily tied to developments in Africa and to the Arab-Israeli conflict. Egypt looks to the United States for military and economic assistance, especially for assistance in strengthening Egypt's defensive capability. At the same time, however, Egypt is particularly sensitive to any encroachments on its sovereignty and has not been receptive to American efforts to acquire base rights in Egypt. Egypt has also declined the prospect of NATO membership, at least for the time being, thus keeping its nonaligned option open.

A possible spinoff of the Iranian Revolution might be an Egyptian rapproachment with the Arab Gulf states and a Gulf security role for Egypt. Following the Iranian Revolution Egypt has repeatedly offered to defend the Gulf states from Iranian actions. In September 1979 Sadat offered military aid to Bahrain to counter any Iranian attempt to annex the island nation. In April 1980 the *Arab News* in Jeddah, citing the Kuwait News Agency, reported that Egyptian State Minister for Foreign Affairs Butros Ghali stated: "In case of aggression, Egypt would rush to the aid of the Gulf states under the Arab Collective Security Pact of 1950 which was later signed by several Arab Gulf states."[17] He also added: "Of course Egypt will help only if asked to do so."[18]

Sharing a common interest in controlling revolutionary pressures, Egypt could possibly move closer to Saudi Arabia, Iraq, and other Arab Gulf states. Current criticism of the Camp David peace process notwithstanding, such a rapproachment could be in the offing. Not only has Iraq received arms assistance from Egypt in early 1981, but in March 1981 President Saddam Hussein in a speech reported by the Iraqi News Agency included Egypt with other Arab states that Iraqi forces could protect against aggression.[19]

REVOLUTION AND SECURITY

The reactions of Saudi Arabia, Iraq, and Egypt to the revolutionary pressures spawned by the Iranian Revolution have been somewhat similar. Each state has shown distinct efforts to promote the legitimacy of their government, while tightening internal security. All three states have sought to promote political participation, but their steps have varied and have been carefully measured. Saudi Arabia and Egypt have stressed the role of Islam and Islamic law in their societies. Iraq, while maintaining a reverence for Islam, has focused attention upon nationalism, Arab unity, and the accomplishments of the Baath revolution. All three states have moved to improve the material well-being of their masses, though Egypt's successes appear fragile. Saudi Arabia and Iraq have each emphasized nonalignment. Egypt, though looking to the United States for support, has stopped short of permitting American bases in Egypt and has kept its nonalignment option open.

With regard to the common interests in stability shared by Saudi Arabia, Iraq, and Egypt, the Iranian Revolution could serve to move these three key Middle Eastern states toward increased cooperation to combat revolutionary pressures.

NOTES

1. See Youssef M. Ibrahim, "New Data Link Takeover With Islamic Political Discontent," *New York Times,* 25 February 1980, p. A-6.
2. *Washington Post,* 2 March 1980, p. A-25.
3. *Arab News* (Jeddah), 18 October 1979, p. 1.
4. The SSF is a 2,000-3,000 man security force responsible to the Deputy Minister of the Interior, Prince Ahmad. See Nigel Harvey, "Fahd Accepts Delay in Arms Sales," *Guardian* (Manchester), 30 April 1981, p. 7.
5. *Wahsington Post,* 25 May 1975, p. A-15.
6. See "Gulf Security Document," *The Middle East* (London), No. 75, January 1981, pp. 16-17.
7. *Ibid.*
8. *Ibid.*
9. "Gulf Unity: Building in Progress," *The Middle East* (London), No. 78, April 1981, pp. 8-9.
10. *Washington Post,* 27 September 1979, p. A-26.
11. For text of "Doctrine," see "United Arab Response to Current Challenges," *Iraq Today,* 5, (1-15 February 1980), pp. 2-3.
12. See Ann Elizabeth Mayer, "Islamicizing Egypt's Laws: A Go-Slow Policy?" *Middle East Executive Reports,* 3 (September 1980), pp. 3, 17-18.
13. See Louise Leif, "Egyptians wonder how long Sadat can keep wages up, prices down," *Christian Science Monitor,* 5 May 1981, p. 4.
14. *Ibid.*
15. *Ibid.*
16. Edward Cody, "Sadat Presses Bill to Punish Dissent," *Washington Post,* 21 February 1980, A-27.
17. *Arab News* (Jeddah, 6 April 1980, p. 4.
18. *Ibid.*
19. *Washington Post,* 30 March 1981, p. A-26.

*The directors of the Institute of Middle Eastern
and African Affairs
Welcome the submission of manuscripts
relevant to the Middle East and Africa.
Manuscripts submitted for publication
must be prepared in double-spaced typescript.
Footnotes should be placed at the end of the text.
It is essential that three copies of the manuscript be submitted.*

**Institute of Middle Eastern and North
African Affairs (Inc.)**

**P. O. Box 1674
Hyattsville, Maryland 20788
U.S. A.**